Affair at Captina Creek

by
Harry G. Enoch

HERITAGE BOOKS
2009

HERITAGE BOOKS
AN IMPRINT OF HERITAGE BOOKS, INC.

Books, CDs, and more—Worldwide

For our listing of thousands of titles see our website at
www.HeritageBooks.com

Published 2009 by
HERITAGE BOOKS, INC.
Publishing Division
100 Railroad Ave. #104
Westminster, Maryland 21157

Copyright © 1999 Harry G. Enoch

Other books by the author:

Grimes Mill, Kentucky Landmark on Boone Creek, Fayette County
In Search of Morgan's Station and "The Last Indian Raid in Kentucky"

Cover illustration adapted from drawing by
Herbert Sherlock. Courtesy of Archival Services,
University of Akron, Akron, Ohio

All rights reserved. No part of this book may be reproduced or transmitted in any form or by any means, electronic or mechanical, including photocopying, recording or by any information storage and retrieval system without written permission from the author, except for the inclusion of brief quotations in a review.

International Standard Book Numbers
Paperbound: 978-0-7884-1112-0
Clothbound: 978-0-7884-8095-9

To Brenda
who has endured all with patience, love and understanding

Table of Contents

Illustrations	vii
Preface	ix
PART I: BACKGROUND AND OVERVIEW	1
Harmar's Defeat, October 1790	3
Indian War, Early 1791	
I. Lower Ohio Valley	6
II Upper Ohio Valley	8
The Frontier Rangers	12
Massacre of the Crow Sisters	22
Battle of Captina Creek	26
Baker's Fort and Captina Creek, Then and Now	32
PART II: AN INQUIRY INTO THE CAPTINA AFFAIR	47
Analysis	49
In Perspective	71
Biographical Sketches	77
PART III: DOCUMENTARY RECORDS	103
Accounts of the Captina Affair	105
David Shepherd	105
York General-Advertiser	106
John Dailey	108
John Shoptaw	110
John Yoho	113
John Bain	114
Daniel Bain	115
John McDonald	117
George McKiernan	120
Samuel Tomlinson	124
William Harrod, Jr.	128
Martin Baker	129

Daniel Wire	132
Wills de Hass	132
Ezekiel Boggs	136
Jeremiah Hollister	138
Samuel Hedges	142
Frontier Rangers, 1791	144
Ohio County Militia	144
Washington County Militia	146
Notes	147
Index	189

Illustrations

Upper Ohio Valley in 1791	2
Counties of Southwest Pennsylvania and Northwest Virginia	13
Frontier Ranger and Shawnee Indian	23
Southwest Washington County, Pennsylvania, and Ohio County, Virginia, May 1791	24
Crow Sisters Massacre	25
Field Trip to Marshall County, West Virginia, and Belmont County, Ohio	33
Map of Cresap Bottom Showing the Site of Baker's Fort	34
North Bank of Captina Creek	35
Captina Creek Near the Battle Site	35
Powhatan Point	36
View of Northern End of Cresap Bottom	36
Portrait of General Duncan McArthur	61
Site of the Battleground on Captina Creek, May 2, 1791	62

Preface

In 1791 open war broke out on the western frontier, as Native Americans made one last attempt to rid the Ohio River Valley of white settlers. The valley filled with the smoke of burning cabins and ran with the blood of pioneer families. The previous October, General Josiah Harmar had led a campaign against the confederated nations of the Northwest Territory, and his army was badly beaten near present-day Fort Wayne, Indiana. Now, brimming with confidence after Harmar's defeat, Little Turtle's Miami, Blue Jacket's Shawnee and their allies were striking white settlements all across the trans-Allegheny frontier. Families throughout the valley were leaving their homes and retreating to nearby forts for safety, a practice the settlers had hoped would end after the Revolutionary War. In western Virginia and Pennsylvania, new forts were thrown up, county militias were called out, and Ranger companies were sent to frontier outposts.

In January 1791 the Northwest nations unleashed a series of attacks against the white settlements on the west side of the Ohio River. By March the war had expanded east and south of the river. Border warfare continued on the frontier throughout the summer and fall of 1791. With the British fanning the flames and ineffectual support provided by Virginia, Pennsylvania, and the federal government, war ran on for four years. It finally ended with General "Mad Anthony" Wayne's victory at the Battle of Fallen Timbers in 1794 and was followed a year later by the treaty of Greenville. This book describes the first few months of the border war, elaborating on events that led up to the battle of Captina, an engagement between the Shawnee and a militia company from Washington County, Pennsylvania.

The militia on the western frontier were referred to as Rangers, so called because they formed "ranging companies" that patrolled the hinterland searching for signs of Indian war parties. They formed an important element in the security of the widely scattered settlements. In May 1791 a company of Washington County Rangers set out from Ryerson's Station in search of a party of Indians that had killed three daughters of Jacob Crow. Ryerson's Station was located on the Dunkard fork of Wheeling, about five miles upstream from Crow's Fort (in present-day Greene County, Pennsylvania). The Rangers pursued the Indians west to the Ohio River. At Baker's Fort (in present-day Marshall County, West Virginia), the company crossed the river and met a party of Shawnee in battle near the banks of Captina Creek (the site is now within the little town of Powhatan Point in Belmont County, Ohio). That day the Shawnee bested the whites in a hard-fought contest that left both sides bloodied. The most illustrious participant in this fray was Duncan McArthur, who later became governor of the state of Ohio.

Captina Creek, a minor military engagement and now nearly forgotten, was nevertheless a signal battle in the border war. Here the Indians fought with a discipline and determination they had seldom displayed in previous encounters. Here was a manifestation that their objective was not merely harassment, but rather the destruction and eradication of frontier settlements. Shawnee, Miami, Delaware, Mingo and other nations were allied in a mission to drive the whites out of the Ohio valley and, if possible, back over the Alleghenies. The concern this incident generated at the time is indicated by the fact that following the battle, the county lieutenant, David Shepherd, sent a personal envoy to the capital to give the U.S. Secretary of War, Henry Knox, an account of the action. The meeting was followed by Secretary Knox's acknowledgment of "the deplorable situation of the inhabitants" and his promise to supply arms and ammunition from the federal government.

Most of the published material relating to the border wars has concentrated on the exploits of notable figures on the frontier, men like George Rogers Clark, Simon Kenton and Daniel Boone. Another focus has been familiar incidents, such as the battle of

Point Pleasant, the siege of Fort Henry (Wheeling), or the burning of Colonel William Crawford at the stake near Sandusky. Other than for these major figures and events, few detailed studies of border incidents—major or minor—have been undertaken.

This work began as an investigation of the circumstances surrounding the Captina affair and the sequence of events of the battle. A variety of sources are available: Several contemporary reports mention the incident; a number of the participants left their recollection of events; and a few authors have constructed accounts based partly upon personal knowledge and partly upon oral tradition. In trying to reconstruct the sequence of events at Captina and sort out the discrepancies in various accounts, one encounters several interesting historical problems: Who were the informants for the published reports on the battle? How reliable are they? Exactly when did the battle take place? What events immediately preceded the battle? What circumstances brought a Ranger company from Pennsylvania to Ohio County, Virginia? Who were the Indians and militiamen involved? What were the consequences of the battle for each side? As it turns out, each of these questions may be answered with a reasonable degree of confidence. The following narrative examines these and other issues surrounding the battle of Captina Creek.

Part I presents the background leading up to the Captina affair; Part II is a detailed reconstruction and analysis of the battle; and Part III is a collection of all available accounts of the battle to which is appended a listing of militiamen of Ohio County and Washington County taken from pay rolls and muster rolls of 1791. End material includes Notes to the text with references to the sources used in preparing this work.

A diligent effort has been made to recreate the battle from primary records. Use of secondary sources and the author's speculation have been clearly indicated. This narrative makes no attempt to provide a modern sociological perspective. My purpose was to piece together the story from available evidence in order to present a factual account—without bias to whites or Native Americans—of these nearly-forgotten events. No moral judgments are offered or are intended. The author has a scholarly interest in and a deep respect for Native Americans. This account is intended to honor their memories, as well as their white-skinned adversaries.

In transcribing original documents, minor changes were made to improve readability: abbreviations were spelled out; capitalization was added, when needed, at the beginning of sentences; and some punctuation was added for clarity. Otherwise wording and spelling are unchanged. Brackets indicate additions to the original, and ellipses indicate omissions.

I would like to thank the following individuals for providing source materials and for their insightful comments on portions of the manuscript: Lee Bain, Karen Bridgeman, Nancy Carter, Jennifer Enoch, Mary Jane Henney, Naomi Lowe, Andy Morris, Russell Morris, Evan Rogerson, Carolyn and Victor Rutter, Phyllis Slater, Clair John Thompson and Nancy Tomlinson. I would like to thank Lee Ashlin, my editor at Heritage Books, for his able assistance. I am grateful for the assistance provided by the staff at the University of West Virginia Library, West Virginia Collection, Morgantown, WV; Moundsville Public Library, Moundsville, WV; Greene County Historical Society Library, Waynesburg, PA; Washington County Historical Society Library, Washington, PA; Citizens Library, Washington, PA; Ohio Historical Society Library and Archives, Columbus, OH; Cincinnati Historical Society Library and Public Library of Cincinnati and Hamilton County, Cincinnati, OH; University of Kentucky Library, Special Collections, Lexington, KY; Filson Club, Louisville, KY; and Kentucky Historical Society Library and Kentucky Department for Libraries and Archives, Frankfort, KY.

PART I

BACKGROUND AND OVERVIEW

Affair at Captina Creek

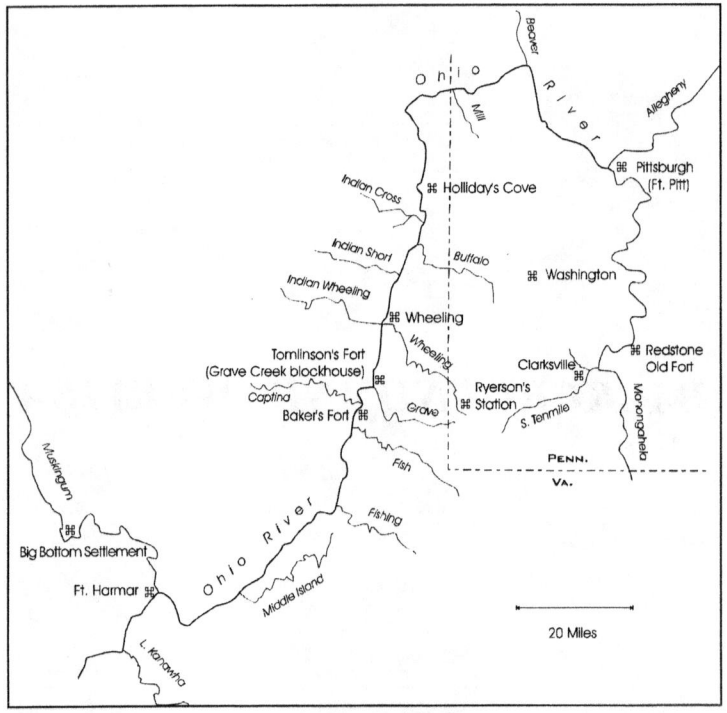

Upper Ohio Valley in 1791

Harmar's Defeat
October 1790

In the Treaty of Paris (1783) which ended the Revolutionary War, England ceded to the United States her claims to the territory that now encompasses five states—Ohio, Indiana, Illinois, Michigan and Wisconsin. The fate of the Native Americans inhabiting that region was not addressed. While the Iroquois League had been effectively destroyed by the war, the tribes of the Old Northwest[1] did not consider themselves a conquered people. The new government of the United States was anxious to enter into peace treaties with the natives, but the western tribes were not interested. At first, the Shawnee refused even to meet with the American commissioners. Finally, a number of agreements were signed relinquishing U.S. claims to a large portion of the Northwest Territory, but as these treaties were signed by chiefs who could not speak for all the tribes, they were repudiated.[2] The uproar over treaty-making helped bring the tribes together and cemented the confederacy, of which the Shawnee and Miami emerged as the dominant forces.

After the war, the Ohio River became a highway to the "promised land," as settlers poured into newly opened country west of the continental divide and the towering Allegheny mountains. During this time, the Ohio nations and their Cherokee neighbors to the south joined to waylay flatboats coming down river, burn isolated cabins, and kill hunters, surveyors and anyone else caught unprotected. The problem was most severe in Kentucky (then part of Virginia), which counted a population of nearly 75,000 by 1790.[3] Sporadic incidents also occurred along the upper Ohio River. Whites responded to these assaults by mounting retaliatory raids against Indian towns. The practice, however, was expressly prohibited with the passage of the Northwest Ordinance in 1787. The ordinance stated that Indian lands "shall never be invaded or disturbed, unless in just and lawful wars authorized by Congress." With the Ohio River serving as a token border, Indian raids across the river continued, and so did retaliatory raids by whites.

In April 1788, Rufus Putnam, a Revolutionary War hero from Massachusetts, led a a group of forty-eight men down river to the mouth of the Muskingum and—under a charter to the Ohio Company—there established the first permanent settlement in Ohio at Marietta (then called Campius Martius).[4] This was followed in November by Benjamin Stites's settlement at Columbia, in December by Matthias Denman and others at Losantiville (later renamed Cincinnati), and in February by John Cleve Symmes at North Bend.[5] This bold trespass of their homelands infuriated the Indians and drew swift retaliation from the confederacy.

As the level of hostilities escalated sharply, the western settlements received little support from the eastern states.[6] Those states directly affected—Virginia and Pennsylvania—were reluctant to send regular troops to the border to prevent incursions against their frontiers. Virginia's governor, Beverly Randolph, went so far as to rebuke the local militias for their "defensive" raids. On March 10, 1790, Randolph wrote to the county lieutenants of the western counties:

> The Governor of the Continental Western Territory [Arthur St. Clair] has given the executive [President Washington] information of incursions having been made by parties from this state upon the tribes of Indians in amity with the United States. . . . Should it be necessary on any occasion to order out parties to repel attack of an enemy within the limits of the state, you will issue the most positive orders that no such party shall under any pretense whatever enter into the territory . . . of any Indian tribe.[7]

It soon became apparent to the federal government that its laws and treaty-making efforts were not going to bring about a permanent peace in the West. In response to the continuing western clamor, President Washington ordered the governor of the

Background and Overview

Northwest Territory, Arthur St. Clair, to raise an army from Virginia and Pennsylvania for an expedition against the Ohio nations. In late September of 1790, General Josiah Harmar[8] set out from Fort Washington (Cincinnati) with 1,453 men: his army consisted of 320 regulars bolstered by two battalions of militiamen from Kentucky and one from Pennsylvania. The Indians—led by Little Turtle (Miami) and Blue Jacket (Shawnee)—were well aware of Harmar's approach. After burning several deserted villages on the Maumee River (near present-day Fort Wayne, Indiana), Harmar's troops were badly beaten in two separate engagements. In early November the army limped back into Fort Washington, having lost nearly two hundred men. Putting the best possible light on a dreadful state of affairs, Harmar wrote to Secretary of War Henry Knox on November 23:

> No interruption whatever was offered by the enemy on our return, a convincing proof this, of their having received a blow which they felt. I flatter myself good consequences will be the result. . . . Our loss can be repaired; theirs is irreparable.[9]

Harmar neglected to mention that he never engaged his main body in the fighting, did not use his artillery, and lost most of his military equipment and supplies on the retreat. Governor St. Clair was even more enthusiastic than Harmar in his report to Knox:

> I have the pleasure to inform you of the entire success of General Harmar at the Indian towns on the Miami [Maumee] and St. Joseph Rivers, of which he has destroyed five in number, and a very great quantity of corn. . . .[10]

In reality, while the Indians had suffered some losses, they were hardly defeated. The blow merely served to increase their anger and unite the tribes. Harmar had stirred the hornets' nest.[11]

Indian War, Early 1791
I. Lower Ohio Valley

In spite of Harmar's claims of success for his campaign, the result was a firestorm unleashed on the frontiers as the western nations joined to declare war on white settlements.[12] In his epic history of the frontier, *The Winning of the West*, Theodore Roosevelt declared that after Harmar's defeat

> Along the Ohio people lived in hourly dread of tomahawk and scalping knife; the attacks fell unceasingly on all the settlements from Marietta to Louisville.[13]

Traditionally, the Indians had waited until spring to begin their campaigns, but for the unfortunates on the Ohio side of the river, the onslaught in 1791 began before the winter snows had melted.

The most sanguine affair occurred at Big Bottom on the Muskingum River (about thirty miles upstream from Rufus Putnam's settlement at Marietta). Here the previous autumn, thirty-six men had erected a few cabins and a large blockhouse for defense and had brought out their families. They had done so in spite of the fact that

> Those best acquanted with the Indians . . . had little doubt that the Indians were preparing to Commence hostilities, [and] strongly opposed the settlement going out that fall.[14]

Just before dark on the cold evening of January 2, Indians descended upon the settlement while the occupants were eating supper and took it entirely by surprise. Those not killed were carried off into captivity. Only two young boys managed to escape. The next day a relief party found twelve bodies in the smoking ruins.[15] The determined settlers who remained on the Muskingum built a defensive structure—Fort Freye—about six miles east of Big Bottom. The triangular fort was completed in early March and on March 11 was attacked by a party of Wyandot and Delaware. The fort was garrisoned with forty men at the time, and the attack was thwarted.[16]

By early 1791, Indians were seemingly a constant presence near Cincinnati, staging numerous raids and killing several men. In January, a war party attacked a surveying company out near Dunlap's Station at Colerain. All escaped to the small fort except Abner Hunt, who was captured. The Indians invested the station, manned at the time by U.S. troops, Colonel Kingsbury commanding. Some reports placed the Indians' number at four to five hundred—no doubt somewhat exaggerated. When the commander refused to surrender, the Indians subjected Hunt to prolonged torture and finally burned him within sight of the station. After two days the Indians gave up the siege and quietly retired.[17] About the first of May, Indians killed two men from Covalt's Station, a picketed fort with eight to ten cabins. Abraham Covalt and Joseph Hinkle were out cutting logs near the station when they were shot and then scalped by a raiding party.[18] Dunlap's Station was twelve miles up the Big Miami River; Covalt's Station was twelve miles up the Little Miami.[19]

By spring, the Ohio River had become a gauntlet to run for would-be settlers, as the Indians attempted to block the major artery of encroachment into their native lands. On March 22 they attacked a boat about forty miles up river from Maysville, Kentucky, killing nineteen. Four days later two more boats were taken—on the first, the French captain was killed and all on board captured; on the second, all were put to death. One of the fiercest encounters occurred about ten miles upstream from the mouth of the Scioto, where the Shawnee attacked two separate parties descending the river on the morning of March 24. Captain William Hubbell's party was intercepted by several canoes carrying twenty-five to thirty warriors each. Hubbell and his well-armed force were able to repulse the attack and avoid being driven into the shore, where several hundred more Indians were waiting. Of the nine men in Hubbell's boat, three were killed and four were seriously wounded, including Hubbell. The boat following closely behind Hubbell had two killed before they made it through. The Shawnee did succeed in capturing several canoes that were accompanying Hubbell down river. One of them carried Jacob Greathouse, who seventeen years earlier had instigated the murder of Chief Logan's family. Those in the canoes were quickly killed or taken captive, except for Greathouse and his wife, who were slowly tortured to death on the river bank.[20]

II. Upper Ohio Valley

The Indians were active in the upper Ohio valley as well. In January, although they had not yet crossed the river, they managed to capture John Lamasters on the Ohio side and kill him. David Shepherd, the county lieutenant of Ohio County, Virginia, described Lamasters' death, which occurred about eight miles north of Wheeling:

> On the 16th of this Instant [January] a Certain John Lamasters was kiled by the Indians and about twelve Horses Stolen Near the Mouth of Short Creek, on The west Side of the Ohio, and The people much allarmed, as by Every account we Can Expect Nothing but an Indian War. The Inhabitants on the East Side of the Ohio Seem to be in the Same Situation. . . .

Shepherd went on in his dispatch to plea for military supplies and to call for additional militia to garrison and patrol the frontier.

> As The Supply That was allowed us under the Last orders That I Received Doth not appear anyways adiquate to the present Immergancy, I thought it my Duty to Inform you of the Same, as the Communication betwen us and General Harmer Becomes Dangerous and we Can Expect no Relief from That quarter. I Expect That Before This time you have heard of The Murders Done at Muskingum [Big Bottom]. It Seems to be the Opinion of the Officers of this County that it would Require a full

Company of Rangers at least to be of any Service to this County.[21]

On January 28, nine or ten men from the Short Creek area of Ohio County were attacked while out hunting in Indian country—on Stillwater Creek, about forty miles northwest of Wheeling. Indians struck the hunters' camp during the night as the men were sleeping. One of the men, James Boggs, was shot through the hip and could not get away, but the others made their escape. The Indians scalped Boggs and made off with the hunters' guns, horses and furs.[22] Ohio County leaders began to stir, and Colonel Shepherd soon had occasion to write the governor of Pennsylvania to describe this and yet another unfortunate incident:

> About the first of March last, a number of Indians came down to the Banks of the Ohio River, in the Western Territory, and killed in the most cruel manner four of our Citizens and took two prisoners [Riley family], and a short time before having taken a great number of skins and furs from a party of our men [Boggs party], who went a few miles over the Ohio, only with a view of hunting. I thought at that time it was necessary to send out a small party in order to prevent those Indians from doing any further mischief; this party I sent out discovered the track of the Indians but a small distance from where they committed the murder.[23]

Shepherd's letter describes a Delaware raid at Francis Riley's cabin, which was located near the mouth of Indian Cross Creek. During a warm spell in February, the Indians first surprised Mrs. Riley while she was out making sugar. They tied her to a tree and then went in search of the others. Two sons and a son-in-law, John Schemerhorn, were killed while out working in a field; one daughter was killed in the cabin; and two daughters were taken prisoner and carried to Detroit. Another son, Moses, escaped to nearby Carpenter's Station. The mother was able to get away, too, before the Indians returned to the cabin for her.[24] The company Shepherd sent out in search of the attackers was led by Samuel Brady.[25] Brady's scouts were soon on the trail.

> Brady and Company has discovered the trail of they suppose two hundred Indians which they left in the forks of Indian Cross Creek about ten miles from the river last knight. They Expect them to Strike some of the Stations on the other side the river this knight. We have sent to Washington [Pennsylvania], but would wish you to Send on all Quarters that you can get any men. If we can get men enough to cross the river tomorrow and fight them we may stop their Carrear but otherwise god knows the event.... We are very Scarce of guns and Scarce any amunition.[26]

The eastward-flowing Indian Cross Creek runs into the Ohio River about three miles downstream from Steubenville, Ohio. Entering nearly opposite is the westward-flowing Cross Creek. There are several other creeks which empty into the Ohio River from opposite sides and had the same name, except that the creek on the Ohio side was preceded by "Indian," since it was then on the Indian side of the river (e.g., Wheeling Creek and Indian Wheeling Creek, Short Creek and Indian Short Creek).

Brady's scouts were joined by two Ranger companies, those of Captain Thomas Mills[27] from Ohio County and Captain Francis McGuire[28] from Washington County. Now thirty strong, they tracked the Indians to the mouth of Beaver Creek and on March 9 took their revenge. The Rangers surprised the encamped Delaware, killing four. The others escaped but left behind some of the plunder that had been taken at the Rileys. A dispute immediately arose when white traders in the area claimed that those killed were "friendly Indians." The prominent Seneca chief, Cornplanter, wrote to President Washington to protest the murder of his "good honest people."[29] Several of the Allegheny County leaders complained as well, their greatest concern being that the attack would provoke retaliation by the Indians. One wrote that

> This ill-timed stroke, to say no worse, has greatly alarmed the settlements opposite Beaver. They have left their houses along the river for some distance.... Should the Indians revenge this injury done them on our frontier, which it is more than probable they will, that thriving settlement on Racoon will break up and fly a considerable distance into the interior part of the country.[30]

Beaver Creek flows into the Ohio River from the north, twenty-nine miles downstream from Pittsburgh. Raccoon Creek empties into the Ohio from the south, three miles below Beaver.[31] The area just north of the Allegheny and Ohio rivers in Allegheny County was called "the Depreciation Tract." The land there had been set aside by Pennsylvania for the state's Revolutionary War veterans to purchase using the "depreciated" currency with which they had been paid.

The Indians' revenge for the Beaver Creek incident was not long in coming. Allegheny County's greatest fears were realized, as the reprisals fell within only a few miles of Pittsburgh. General Presley Neville[32] described two raids that took place before the end of March:

> On the 18th Instant [March] one man was killed and three Prisoners taken from about four Miles above Pittsburgh on the Alleghany Shore, and on the 23d Instant Thirteen Men, Women and Children, mostly the latter, were killed about fifteen Miles above Pittsburgh on the same river.... The settlement on the depreciation Tract, amounting to about Forty or Fifty Families, has fled to a Man, and many on the Ohio have moved to more interior Situations.[33]

Colonel John Wilkins, Jr.,[34] writing directly to the governor, expressed concern that the frontiers would be depopulated:

> The Indians have committed considerable depradations on the people living on the west side of the Allegheney river, which has caused our frontier people, for an extent of fifty miles, to fly. They have abandoned their farms, their stock and their furniture, and fled with utmost precipitation.[35]

Even allowing for a bit of exaggeration to impress the governor, it seems that there was danger of the panic becoming general, and with some justification. Large parties of Indians appeared to be converging on the upper Ohio. Several attacks had already occurred—the most recent ones, on the east side of the river. The Indians were getting bolder day by day, and the "season" had only begun.

The Frontier Rangers

By February, Pennsylvania county leaders had begun to address the prospect of renewed Indian hostilities. Their situation was somewhat different from neighboring Virginia. Although western Pennsylvania had suffered in Dunmore's War (1774) and was repeatedly threatened during the Revolutionary War (1775-1783), circumstances there changed after the line was run between Pennsylvania and Virginia. From the time settlement began in the late 1760s until the boundary issue was resolved in 1780, this corner of Pennsylvania was known as the "disputed territory," an area claimed by both states. During that time, Virginia, with policies and land laws that strongly encouraged settlement, made the more aggressive claim. Three Virginia counties—Ohio, Monongalia and Yohogania—had been established (1776) and were holding court. Land was being settled and surveyed under Virginia claims. Virginia also was supporting a sizable frontier militia for defense of the region and was garrisoning Fort Pitt with regular troops. Pennsylvania, on the other hand, was actively

Background and Overview

discouraging settlement during the war years, and its militia took little part in the defense of the disputed territory.

The militia system had been in place since colonial days. Following the American Revolution, states authorized their counties to select a county lieutenant with the rank of colonel. County lieutenants were responsible for enlisting, drilling and ordering out troops from the able-bodied male population. In spite of the fact that these troops, with their limited arms, training and discipline, were often less effective than regular army units, the militia played an important, if not critical, role on the frontier during the Revolutionary War.

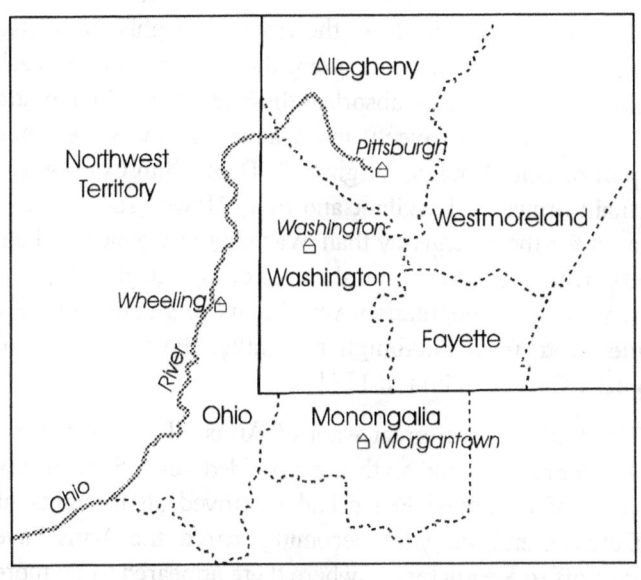

Counties of Southwest Pennsylvania and Northwest Virginia

Virginia, which had provided most of the troops for the wilderness war, gave up her claims to the disputed territory in the boundary agreement of 1780. The area now became a part of Pennsylvania. Two counties—Washington (1781) and Allegheny

(1788)—were established in the southwest corner. The local militiamen, many of whom had migrated there from Virginia, simply took the oath of allegiance to their new state and continued in service. By 1790 the population of the Washington County had swelled to nearly 24,000; Indian raids into the interior had nearly ceased; and steps had been taken to reduce, and eventually dissolve, the militia.

A major factor contributing to the relative tranquillity in Washington County was the location of the Virginia-Pennsylvania border. After running the western boundary, a narrow strip of land was left between Washington County and the Ohio River. With this area acting as a buffer, the county was no longer in the first line of assault. In 1791 the frontier roughly paralleled the Ohio River. The settlements along the river adjoining Washington County had for years absorbed the brunt of the Indian attacks. This area—less than twenty miles across at the widest point—was part of Ohio County, Virginia.[36] Thus, Ohio County had had to remain armed and vigilant and in 1791 was somewhat better prepared for the emergency than Washington County. Allegheny County, with over three times the area of Washington County and less than half the population, was far more vulnerable. Presley Neville wrote from Pittsburgh recounting the sorry state of the Allegheny County militia in 1791:

> The Militia are in great want of Arms. I do not believe that more than one-sixth are provided for. Five or Six years of continued Peace had destroyed all thoughts of Defence, and the game becoming scarce, the Arms have slipt off to Kentucky . . . where there appeared to be more use for them.[37]

Washington County leaders were well aware of the critical role Ohio County played in their defense. Should the outposts along the river fall, the surrounding settlements would be decimated, and as the surviving families left their homes and fled east, Washington County would be exposed. With the outbreak of war in 1791, Washington County stood ready to assist in the defense of their Virginia neighbors. Preparations were made to send Ranger companies west to outposts on the Ohio River. Self-interest rather than magnanimity dictated this action. The county lieutenant, James Marshel,[38] wrote to Governor Mifflin from the county seat of Washington appraising the situation on the frontier in February and, incidentally, of the material consequences of Harmar's campaign:

> Inclosed is a Return of the Officers elected by the Militia of the different Districts in this County. . . . From the fullest evidence of the hostile intentions of the Indians, I have no doubt but that the service of our Militia will be necessary the ensuing Summer. Our situation on the frontier at this time is truly alarming. The late Expedition under the comand of General Harmar has had a very different effect from what was expected. The Indians appear elated with their success on that occasion and are roused by a Spirit of Resentment. It is evident that nothing prevents their crossing the Ohio River but the inclemency of the Season. . . . They have . . . committed frequent murders on the west side of the River and had the Insolence, after killing a family a few days ago on the bank of the River, to call to the people on this side . . . "that it would be their turn next and that they would not leave a Smoking Chimney on this side the Alliganey Mountains."

Marshel then went on to speak of the cooperation between Washington and Ohio counties and to add a plea for action:

> I have also thought it my Duty to state to your Excellency our apprehensions of Danger, that speedy and effectual measures may be taken, either by the General [federal] or State government, for the protection and safety of our frontier. Offensive War is in my humble opinion the most eligable. This country at present abounds with the Necessary supplies for an army. . . . I have only to add,

that such is our sense of Danger, that the joint application from this and Ohio County to the General Government has been forwarded by express at the expence of a few Individuals.[39]

No doubt many westerners shared James Marshel's sentiments. It appeared that the military leaders were attempting to portray Harmar's campaign as a great victory. This notion was inhibiting the bold, decisive actions needed to stem the present tide of bloodshed brought on, ironically, by the "great victory." The westerners spoke their mind on this subject at every opportunity. With a touch of sarcasm, David Redick[40] wrote to the governor in plainer tones of Harmar's defeat:

> It must be the prevailing opinion, from the splendid accounts given by the governor of the Western territory and General Harmar, of the success of our troops in the late expedition, that the hostile tribes have got at best a check and that the frontier people will be in safety. Nothing is further from the fact. With reluctance, indeed, do I dare to contradict the opinion founded on such respectable authority; but . . . the Indians boast of having obtained a victory, and this is further supported by the audacity and daily insolence which the frontiers have, ever since the return of the army, experienced at the hands of Indians.

Redick's letter continued with a description of how Washington County's welfare hinged upon maintaining the security of their western neighbor on the river, namely, Ohio County, Virginia.

> The Dunkard creek and Ten Mile settlements may be secured by the River Ohio being made a line of defence for the people of Virginia; but as their [Virginia's] settlements don't reach so far down the river as to cover these two tracts of country, we are then immediately vulnerable. Up the river our people are settled on the North West side of the river, and who must either fly in on the interior settlements, or fall an easy prey.[41]

The governor forwarded Marshel's and Redick's letters to Secretary Henry Knox at the War Department. The county lieutenants of western Pennsylvania and Virginia received a prompt response. On March 3, Knox wrote to inform them that Congress and the President had acted upon the requests for aid in the West—they ordered the frontier counties to defend themselves!

> Gentlemen—The President of the United States has received your letter of the 19th of last month Stating certain depredations of the Indians. And he has commanded me to inform you that the Congress of the United States, having been deliberating for some time past upon the means which may efectually protect the frontiers, have just concluded thereon. That he [the President] shall take the most vigorous measures to execute the intentions of Congress. That for this purpose men will be required to act offensively. That *it is to be hoped and expected*, that as soon as the conditions shall be made known, *that the hardy yeomanry of the frontier counties will engage readily and chearfully for a short period to act against the Indians* and thereby prevent their depopulating the exposed parts of the county of Ohio. That the governor of the western territory [Arthur St. Clair] who will immediately repair to Fort Pitt, or *the commanding officer of the troops, will have discretionary power to make all necessary arrangements for the temporary defensive protection of the frontier counties which the occasion may require.*[42] (emphasis added)

While hardly the help the counties had requested, at least it was something. Local militia commanders now had "discretionary power" to take whatever measures were necessary to protect the frontiers. This was widely interpreted as a lifting of the ban on raids into Indian territory. No longer would the militia fear rebuke from their own government for pursuing Indian raiding parties into Ohio. Although pursuit across the river had never ceased, at least it would now be legal.

After urging "the hardy yeomanry of the frontier counties" to shoulder their own protection, the Secretary of War followed on March 10 with a detailed plan for calling Ranger companies into service. Under Knox's plan, the Rangers rather than regular army troops would be required to defend the frontiers. The county militia would function as it traditionally had, except that their expenses would be borne by the federal government. In his letter to the county lieutenants, Knox directed the militia to be filled by volunteers "or otherwise," but requested that the counties not burden the government with the expense of calling out "an unnecessary number of men":

> In consideration of the present exposed situation of the county of [Washington, Allegheny, Westmoreland and Ohio] The president of the United States hereby authorizes you to embody at the expence of the United States as many of the militia by voluntary engagements, or otherwise, according to law, as in your judgement the defensive protection of the said county may require.
>
> He is persuaded that from a regard to proper economy, and your own character, you will not call out an unnecessary number of men.
>
> The rangers to be called into service in pursuance of this authority are to be upon the same establishment of pay and rations as the troops of the United States, agreably to the schedule herein enclosed.

The schedule of pay and rations for the U.S. military approved on April 30, 1790, is found in the Virginia *Calendar of State Papers*.[43] A portion of the schedule is reproduced below:

Major	$40 per month	4 rations per day
Captain	$30	3
Lieutenant	$22	2
Ensign	$18	2
Sergeant	$5	1
Private	$3	1

Background and Overview

A "ration" was to consist of

> one pound of beef or three-quarters of a pound of Pork, one pound of bread or flour, Half a gill of Rum or brandy or whiskey, one quart of salt, Two quarts of Vinegar, Two pounds of soap, [and] one pound of candles for every hundred rations.

The Secretary of War's letter went on to delineate additional administrative details. The Rangers would continue to serve under the broad authority of the county lieutenants, who were responsible for equipping, paying and deploying the men:

> The county lieutenants are to make an arrangement for supplying the said rangers with rations, provided each ration shall not exceed the amount of eight cents.
>
> The county lieutenants are also to direct the said rangers to be mustered upon entering and leaving the service, and the officers commanding the said rangers are to make oath to the truth of their muster rolls.
>
> That muster rolls and abstracts for the pay and rations of said rangers are to be made out and certified by the county lieutenants, who are to transmit the same to the War office for examination and payment, and also their powers of attorney to receive the money.
>
> You will report to me and the commanding general of the troops, in writing, the number you may have called out by virtue of this authority, and the arrangements you have made for furnishing them with rations. . . .

After this lengthy expostulation on bureaucratic minutiae, Knox outlined the strategy to be used by the militia. Rangers were directed to stay on the move, scouring the wilderness for signs of the enemy. One could interpret these instructions to mean that the Rangers now had license to do whatever was necessary "to secure the inhabitants":

> You will keep the said rangers in constant activity, in such directions as may best prove to secure the inhabitants, and to give information of the approach of the Indians.[44]

As a general rule, Rangers did not engage in offensive operations and rarely fought in pitched battles. The exception was when volunteer companies were raised to accompany various expeditions against the Indian towns, such as Crawford's campaign in 1782. The primary function of the Rangers was defensive. They were essentially scouting companies and were expected to stay on the go, patrolling a wide area for signs of Indians. When Indian intrusion was detected the Rangers would dispatch riders to the settlements warning residents to be prepared. They frequently used the forts and blockhouses along the Ohio River as a base of operations. These included John Holliday's fort at Holliday's Cove,[45] Wheeling Fort (formerly Fort Henry), Joseph Tomlinson's fort at Grave Creek and John Baker's fort at Fish Creek.

The pioneers were a special brand of American, and Rangers were a special brand of pioneer. The Rangers' duties called for extraordinary qualities, not found in the average citizen. The men who came West seeking to carve a new life out of the wilderness had to improve their land, feed their families and defend them from hostile natives. To quote Francis Parkman, the frontier people of Pennsylvania were "of a rude and hardy stamp, hunters, scouts, rangers, Indian traders, and backwoods farmers, who had grown up with arms in their hands, and been trained under all the influences of the warlike frontier."[46] Although they received little formal military training, the Rangers formed an effective "home guard," and through experience and necessity many units became highly skilled in tracking and engaging their enemy. These skills would be called upon frequently during the Indian war in 1791.

As mentioned in his February letter, James Marshel had already called out the Washington County militia. After receiving authority from the Secretary of War, Colonel Marshel wasted no time in deploying the Rangers. On March 23 he wrote to Colonel Shepherd of Ohio County that he was sending a company to the frontier:

> It is with pleasure I Inform you that I am enabled to Join you in the Mutual Defence of the two Counties, for which purpose [I] have ordered out a Company of Militia, part of which I will send to fish Creek and a number to mill Creek, but will Consult you more particularly before I make any permanent arrangements.[47]

Marshel's strategy is clear. Mill Creek was above Washington County on the north, emptying into the Ohio River near the Pennsylvania state line. Fish Creek lay at the southern extreme of the county, emptying into the Ohio twenty-four miles downstream from Wheeling. From these two locations the Rangers could scout the entire length of the river segment shielding Washington County. One of the scouts appointed by Marshel that March stated that Marshel sent Captain Henry Enoch's company to Fish Creek and Captain Forbis's company thirty-five miles to the north.[48]

After calling out and placing his militia in the field, Marshel wrote to Mifflin on April 11 to inform the governor of the actions he had taken:

> I was authorised by the President of the United States, through the Secretary of War, "to embody at the expense of the United States, as many of the Militia . . . as the defencive protection of this County may require." In consequence of this author, I ordered on duty one Company of Militia for one Month, with the design of embodying within that time, a sufficient number of active Woodsmen [i.e., Rangers—sometimes called "Woods Rangers"] to continue in service six Months . . . for the defence of our frontiers, and which I expect to effect by the 18th Instant [of April]. . . .

One of the companies mustered into service was Captain William Harrod's; his Rangers were posted to Ryerson's Station on the Dunkard fork of Wheeling Creek.[49] Several Ohio County companies were also formed at this time. (See the 1791 rosters of the Frontier Rangers in Part III). Marshel's letter to Mifflin continued:

> We have not yet suffered any damage in this County by the Indians, that I know of. The frontier Inhabitants are, nevertheless, very much alarmed on account of the Murders committed on the Neighbouring frontiers, and several of the frontier settlements in this County have been evacuated before I was authorised to send out any men for their protection.[50]

Marshel still held out hope that prompt decisive action would quell the Indians' initiative and bring a quick end to the hostilities. His optimism would soon be dashed, however, as the Indian war leapt across the Ohio River and spilled into Washington County.

Massacre of the Crow Sisters

The Crow family lived on the Dunkard fork of Wheeling, about five miles downstream from Ryerson's Station. The patriarch, Jacob Crow,[51] had settled on the creek in about 1775 with his growing family. The Crows acquired more property in the area and Jacob built a fort on his farm. They were neighbors of the Wetzels and the Bonnetts.

On May 1, 1791, the Crow family was the victim of a tragedy still remembered as one of the more melancholy incidents in the history of southwest Pennsylvania. That Sunday morning, after visiting a sick neighbor, the four Crow sisters—Susan, Elizabeth (Betsy), Catherine (Katie) and Christina (Tena)—were on their way home. The girls, who ranged in age from eight to sixteen, followed a path down Crabapple Creek, then turned down Dunkard. Near the ford on Dunkard, about two miles from home,

Background and Overview

Frontier Ranger and Shawnee Warrior
Drawings by Herbert Sherlock. Courtesty of Archival Services,
University of Akron, Akron, Ohio

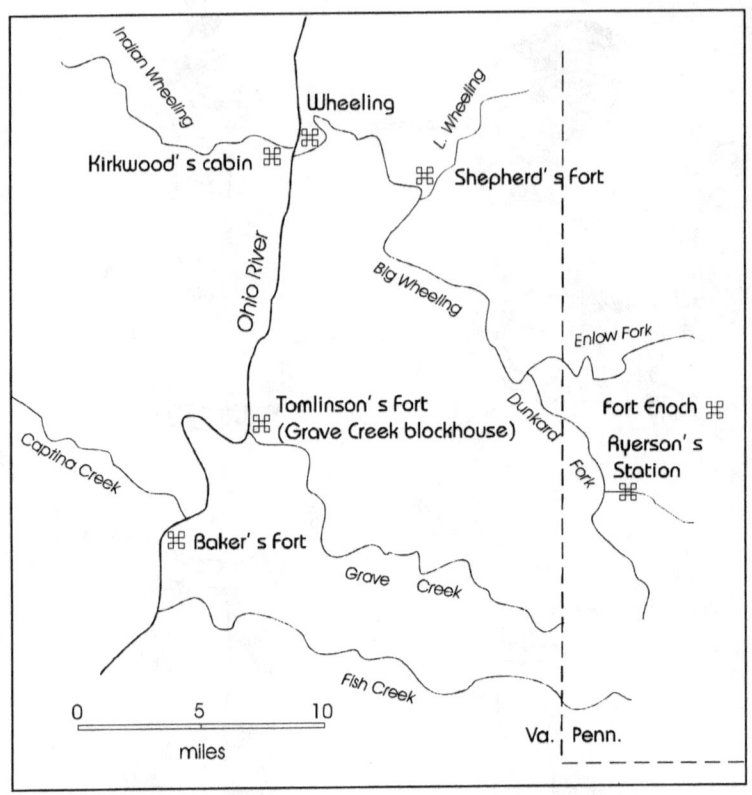

Southwest Washington County, Pennsylvania, and Ohio County, Virginia, May 1791

their brother Michael came by on his horse and offered the youngest a ride. She declined, and Michael rode on to the Crow's fort. As soon as he was out of sight, two Indians and a "white Indian" named Spicer[52] rushed down the creek and surrounded the sisters. They took their captives a little ways off into the woods and began questioning them about the strength of the nearby forts. Anticipating they would be killed if they did not escape, the girls made a run for it. Betsy was tomahawked first. When the Indians left her to begin killing the others, she managed to get away

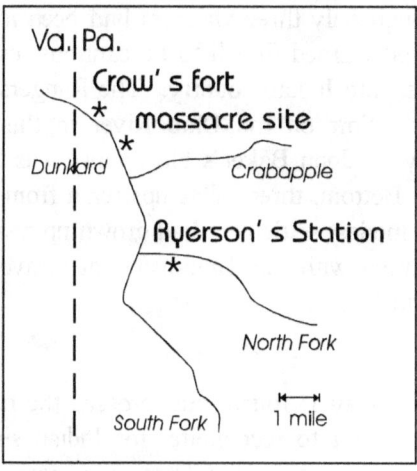

Crow Sisters Massacre

and hide. Tena was bludgeoned with a long rifle by one of the Indians, but she got loose from her captor and ran for home. Katie and Susie were not so fortunate. They were dispatched quickly and scalped. A rescue party did not arrive until the next day. Katie and Susie were both dead. Betsy was found some distance away from the others, still alive. She was brought back to the fort and lived for three days before finally expiring from her wounds. Jacob Crow retreated with his family fifteen miles to the interior, to Lindley's Fort.[53]

The killing had now come to Washington County. Soon the Rangers would be involved in the Indian war.

Battle of Captina Creek

Word of the Crow massacre no doubt reached Captain William Harrod the same day, May 1, at Ryerson's Station. Harrod's son, William Harrod, Jr., recalled that a Ranger detachment under William Enoch was sent out in pursuit of the Indians. Although only three warriors had been involved in the massacre, Harrod warned Enoch to be cautious, especially if he crossed the river into Indian country. The Rangers probably arrived at Baker's Fort on the Ohio River in the afternoon or evening of May 1. John Baker's blockhouse was located at the head of Cresap Bottom, three miles upstream from the mouth of Fish Creek. A modest settlement had grown up near the Bakers, in close association with the Tomlinsons at Grave Creek, eight miles to the north.[54]

Sometime on May 1, four scouts crossed the river in the vicinity of Baker's Fort to reconnoiter for Indian sign. About a mile north of the station on the Ohio side, near the mouth of Captina Creek, the scouts were fired upon by a number of Indians. Adam Miller was killed in the first fire; John Daniels was wounded and taken prisoner. The other two men ran down river to a point nearly across from the fort. Isaac McCowan was killed and scalped on the bank; John Shoptaw managed to swim across the Ohio River to safety. The Indians—Shawnee—taunted the garrison from across the river, daring them to come over. Only a few Indians showed themselves at that time.

Early the next morning, May 2, the Rangers at Baker's Fort crossed the river in pursuit of the Indians. They were led by Abraham Enoch and his party of between fifteen and twenty men including John Baker, Daniel Bain, John Bain, Alexander Boggs,

Background and Overview

John Line, Duncan McArthur, George McColloch, Abraham McCowan, John Sutherland, Ray Vennam, Downing, Dobbins and Hoffman. They picked up the Indians' trail and followed it north to Captina Creek and from there up Captina. About a mile upstream from the mouth they came to a small meadow, later known as "the cove," where the creek makes a bend to the north. They crossed the creek, and just as they started down a narrow ravine, a Shawnee war party opened fire on the column from the high ground. The Indians had purposely created the tracks through the ravine and then doubled back to their concealed positions, where they laid in wait for the Rangers to appear. It was a ploy they had often used with success. The Shawnee, estimated to have numbered between thirty to forty warriors, were led by Charley Wilkey.

Miraculously, no one was killed in the first volley of shooting, and Abraham Enoch was able to keep the company in some sort of order. Each man took cover and began to return fire, but the Indians had the best of it, outnumbering the whites nearly two to one. After several rounds of fire were exchanged by both sides, Enoch took a ball in the breast and expired immediately. The Rangers fell back to obtain better ground, but after suffering additional casualties from the withering fire, they finally had to withdraw. The Indians pressed the attack long enough to block the Rangers' retreat down Captina, forcing them to take an overland route to Grave Creek.

Duncan McArthur, reportedly the youngest man in the company, showed considerable presence in the face of danger. After their commander was killed, McArthur collected what remained of the company and led the retreat back to Grave Creek. Along the way John Baker was seriously wounded and could not continue. He hid under a rock ledge but was discovered and killed by the Indians. George McColloch was wounded in the ankle and, like John Baker, could not keep up with the rest. He made it to the Ohio and concealed himself near the river bank. By one account, McColloch called out in the night, and his friend Ray Vennam, upon hearing him, paddled a canoe across the river and brought him back. After pursuing the fleeing Rangers a short distance, the Indians returned to the field to scalp the dead whites and bury their own dead in a common grave. (Sometime later, this grave was exhumed and found to contain the remains of seven bodies.) The Shawnee took their prisoner, John Daniels, and left the area.

The Rangers reportedly had seven killed (possibly including the scouts from the day before) and several more wounded. In addition to Enoch and Baker, the names of those killed include Abraham McCowan, John Line, and Hoffman (referred to in one account as "a Dutchman"). The next day a party went out from Baker's Fort to collect the dead. They found the bodies of Enoch, Hoffman and Baker badly mangled. The dead were wrapped in white hickory bark, brought back to Baker's and buried in the little graveyard near the fort.

Following the action, on May 6, Colonel Shepherd sent the following dispatch to Secretary Knox at the War Department in Philadelphia[55]:

> Within a few Days past the Indians have made a general attact on us and have killed Seven of our Scouts, Ensign Enox among the killed and Ensign Biggs among the wounded with Several of the privates. They have made attempts to take two of the Blockhouses but have failed and have killed Several of the Inhabitants the Number not known. We have allarms Every Day. The Barer Captain Kirkwood will be more able to give you a perfect account as he was in one of the princable actions to which I refer you. We are without amunition and but a few arms. Every Day Shews New Seens of Cruelty and the appearance of a general invasion.[56]

Shepherd's dispatch refers to two incidents, one on Captina near Baker's Fort where Abraham Enoch ("Enox") was killed and the other at the cabin of Robert Kirkwood,[57] which had occurred the same day or the day before and in which Ensign Joseph Biggs was wounded.

Kirkwood's cabin was located on Indian Wheeling Creek on a hill opposite Wheeling Fort, and he was living there with his family in 1791. Nearby stood an unfinished blockhouse. On the evening of April 30, Biggs with an Ohio County Ranger company of fourteen men were staying overnight at Kirkwood's cabin. A little before daybreak, Indians attacked. They managed to set the cabin on fire but could not take it. One version of the attack was given by Daniel Steenrod, whose brother was in the fight:

> The day before the attack, [Joseph] Biggs, [Briggs] Steenrod and one [John] Walker had been out spying, but discovered no fresh sign. Walker was a New Yorker and declared he would not return to New York till he could carry an Indian's scalp with him as a trophy of his prowess. That evening the men at Kirkwood's thinking there was no danger to be apprehended, caroused and finally went to sleep. The old blockhouse was yet occupied; the new one nearly completed was within a few rods of the old one. The Indians had most likely followed the trail of the spies,[58] stole up and set up some bunches of flax at one corner of the blockhouse, one top of another, so when set on fire the flames would communicate to the roof, and then [they] fired it. The Indians betook themselves to the new blockhouse, through the cracks of which they fired. Kirkwood and his men were instantly at their posts. A ball passed through a port hole and grazed Steenrod and passed through Walker's body, mortally wounding him. Joseph Biggs wounded. As the flames ascended, Kirkwood and Steenrod knocked off the shingles from within and thus saved the blockhouse.[59]

Biggs was wounded early in the fight, and Kirkwood rallied the men. The skirmish was heard a mile away at Wheeling, and those at the fort responded by discharging the cannon. Its loud report echoed across the river and the Indians, realizing that help would soon be on the way, disappeared into the forest. In addition to Biggs, at least five other Rangers at the cabin were wounded:

Elijah Hedges, John Barrett, Joseph Van Meter and John Walker. Walker died the following day.[60] (All of these men except Kirkwood were in the Ohio County militia; see Part III.) The wounds Biggs and Hedges sustained took them out of service for some time. In October both were still under the care of a doctor—Absalom Baird of Washington County.[61] Hedges was "unable to do anything towards supporting himself" and Biggs had "intirely lost the use of his left arm and it does not appear probable that he ever will recover the use of it." Both men later obtained invalid pensions.[62]

The attacks at Captina and Kirkwood's were carried out by different parties of Indians—the former, Shawnee, and the latter, Delaware. The Delaware may have been some of those involved earlier in the attack on the hunters (killing Boggs) and the attack on the Riley family.[63] Shepherd's dispatch to Henry Knox on the battles at Captina and Indian Wheeling was hand delivered by Robert Kirkwood in order to allow him to brief the Secretary of War in person. Knox responded to Governor Randolph with a promise of additional arms and ammunition:

> I have the honor to inform your Excellency, that in consequence of the representation made to me by the Lieutenant of Ohio County, of which the enclosed is a copy, and the verbal communications of Captain Kirkwood stating the deplorable situation of the inhabitants of the said County ... that I have in behalf of the United States ordered that one hundred arms, two barrels of powder, and four hundred weight of lead should be delivered out of the magazine at Fort Pitt to Colonel Shepherd.[64]

Meanwhile, Shepherd took the opportunity to apprise the Virginia governor of the grave conditions in Ohio County. Writing to Beverly Randolph on May 9, he provided a terse summary of the carnage:

> The continued Depredations of Savages upon our frontier Renders our situation truly alarming. . . . During Last week twenty-nine persons have been most Cruelly Murdered.[65]

The western settlements remained imperiled throughout the year of 1791 and for the next two years. A second expedition against the confederacy was launched in the fall of 1791, commanded this time by General Arthur St. Clair. His army was crushed by the allied tribes under the leadership of Little Turtle and Blue Jacket. St. Clair's defeat was even worse than Harmar's, still ranking today as one of the worst defeats ever suffered by the U.S. Army. In 1794 the Indian offensive would finally be crushed by General Wayne in a decisive victory at the battle of Fallen Timbers (near present-day Fort Wayne, Indiana). The militia then began to fade away—the "glory days" of the Rangers were over.

During the border war the Rangers had served an important purpose, defending the frontier and allowing the white settlers to maintain their toehold in the western country. The militia continued as an organized body in Pennsylvania and Virginia for many years, though in a diminished capacity. The role played by the Rangers, however, ceased to exist, as the frontier moved farther west. Washington County quickly forgot the Indian menace and turned to domestic affairs. One matter already at hand in 1794 was the protest against the excise tax on whiskey. It is ironic that that year federal troops were finally sent to Washington County to quell a rebellion—the Whiskey Rebellion. Later, as the last of the frontier Rangers died off or moved away, they became the stuff of legend. Memories of them were touched with romance and nostalgia. The following description of the Rangers' manner of dress serves as a touching tribute to their passing:

> Rome in her proudest days of glory never boasted of a nobler set of men than were those Rangers of the frontier

settlements. In imagination, I see them as in 1793, either standing, walking or reclining at ease; mockasons neatly and securely tied; leather leggings, trimmed on the outside with fringe . . . leather hunting shirt, fringed and confined with a leather belt or girdle, to which were attached the tomahawk and scalping knife. Over these hung the shot-pouch and powder-horn. Occasionally might be seen a blanket thrown carelessly and gracefully over the shoulders. Head surrounded by a cap or turban gracefully wound in folds around it. . . . But where are they now? They repose in silence, and few remain to note their memoirs.[66]

A few men did leave "memoirs" and others took care to collect and preserve them, so that today we have a record of at least some of the Rangers' activities. Fortunately, the Captina affair is included in that number.

Baker's Fort and Captina Creek Then and Now

It requires considerable imagination—amid the profusion of highways, towns and industrial plants—to picture how the unbroken wilderness looked two hundred years ago along the Ohio River. Even the river no longer flows free, but is backed up in a series of elongated lakes (fittingly referred to as "pools") restrained by dams, which are themselves now showing signs of age. I have included with this narrative of the Captina battle the following description of its historical and geographic setting. My intention was to provide readers with an "armchair tour" of the area before launching into a more detailed analysis of the battle itself.

In the fall of 1997, my wife and I took a weekend trip up to Wheeling, West Virginia. I wanted to search for the site of the

Background and Overview

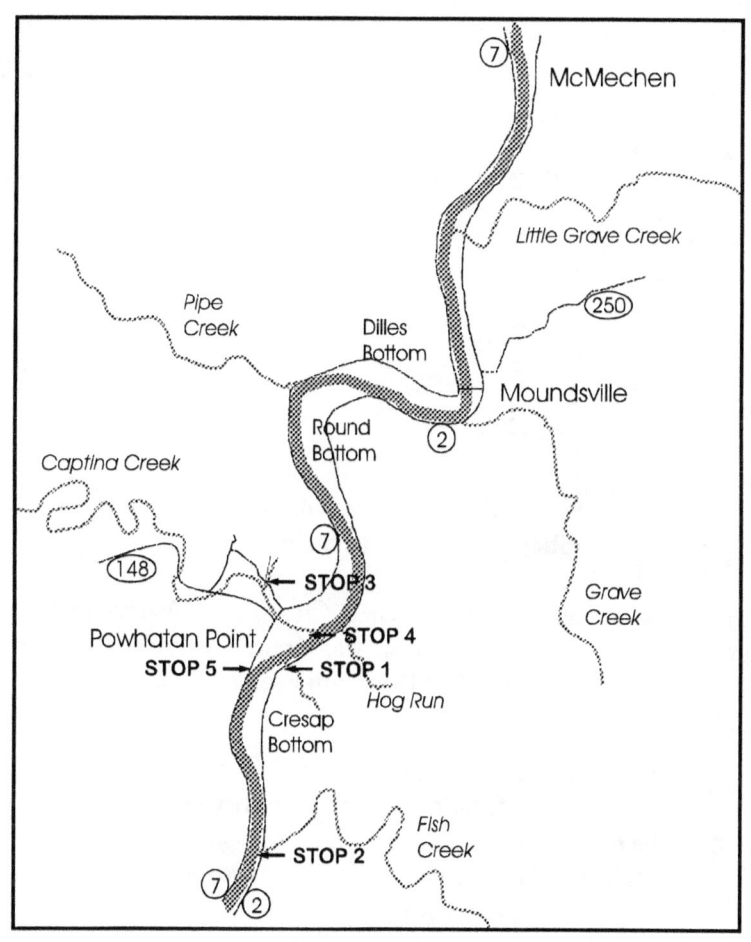

Field Trip to Marshall County, West Virginia, and Belmont County, Ohio

Stop 1, Graveyard Run; **Stop 2**, mouth of Fish Creek on the Ohio River; **Stop 3**, Cove Road, where a gravel road turns off to the right at Cove Run; **Stop 4**, Powhatan Point, at the mouth of Captina Creek; **Stop 5**, west bank of the Ohio River, opposite Graveyard Run. Field notes for these stops are found on pages 37 to 46.

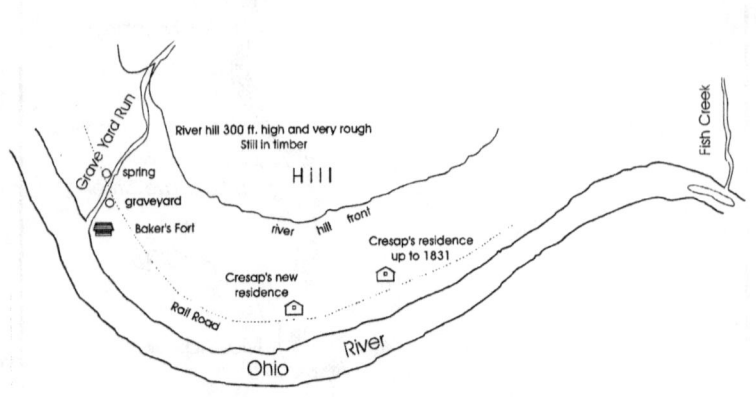

**Map of Cresap Bottom
Showing the Site of Baker's Fort**

Tracing of a map of "Capt. Michael Cresap's 1000 acres of land in Marshall Co. Va." The map was drawn by Friend Cox for Lyman Draper in November 1886. An excerpt from Cox's letter to Draper describes the area:

> Captain Michael Cresaps old and first residence is two miles from the mouth of Fish Creek, but he built a new house and moved in about the year 1831 or 1832, just one-half mile above old place. . . . one mile above Mr. Cresaps House there was a block House or Fort called Bakers Fort situated just below a branch emptying into the Ohio River called Grave Yard Run, because there is or was a burying ground there. Many of the first settlers and Indians fighter are buried there. There was also a fine spring there; the building of the Ohio River Rail Road had destroyed it.

Taken from Draper 14J1-3.

Background and Overview

North Bank (*on left*) of Captina Creek near the battle site. Cove Run empties into Captina just beyond the utility poles. (Stop 3)

View from the north bank of Captina Creek looking south to the "Indian field," now Clair Mar Golf Course. Captina (*barely visible*) runs through the middle of the photograph. (Stop 3)

Affair at Captina Creek

Powhatan Point, where Captina Creek (*on the left*) empties into the Ohio River. (Stop 4)

View of the northern end of Cresap Bottom, looking across the Ohio River from the west bank about one mile southwest of Powhatan Point. Graveyard Run drains the valley between the two hills, just to the left of the two coal silos. (Stop 5)

Background and Overview

old fort and battleground and see how the area differed from the two-century-old descriptions. After spending the night in St. Clairsville—county seat of Belmont County—we set out for Wheeling early on a crisp Saturday morning. Approaching from the west, we descended into the fog-filled valley, crossed the Ohio River on the interstate bridge and headed south on U.S. 250 for Marshall County. The road along the river took us past the boarded up remains of sprawling mills and forges in south Wheeling and Benwood. Just beyond McMechen the divided highway ended, as the road squeezed between the high cliffs and the river at the Narrows, site of the Foreman massacre. On this spot, shortly after the siege of Fort Henry, Captain William Foreman and twenty of his men were killed by Indians (September 27, 1777). South of the Narrows the valley widens unexpectedly on the West Virginia side, in an area known as the Grave Creek flats. Here, between the mouths of Grave Creek and Little Grave Creek, the Tomlinson brothers—Joseph and Samuel—settled in 1771. Joseph Tomlinson platted the town in 1798, calling it Elizabethtown, after his wife. It later became Moundsville, so named for the remarkable Adena burial mounds found in the flats. We hiked to the summit of Grave Creek Mound (250-150 BC) and enjoyed a magnificent view of the riverscape.

Leaving Moundsville we headed west on Route 2 along a bend in the river. The Ohio River cuts into the south bank here—the high cliffs again come nearly down to the water's edge—and the north bank opens into a small alluvial plain known as Dilles Bottom, site of a pioneer blockhouse of that name. The river then comes around and turns south as it sweeps past the mouth of Pipe Creek on the Ohio side and the Round Bottom on the West Virginia side. Here we encountered an historical marker for the "Washington Lands." George Washington admired the setting on his journey down the Ohio in 1770 and made note of it in his journal on October 24:

> [A]bout four Miles lower comes in another [creek] on the East at which place is a path leading to the settlement at

Redstone [this was the mouth of Grave Creek]. About A Mile and half below this again, comes in the Pipe Creek so called by the Indians from a Stone which is found here out of which they make Pipes. Opposite to this (that is on the East side) is a bottom of exceeding Rich Land; but as it seems to lye low, I am apprehensive that it is subject to be overflowed.[67]

Washington apparently got over his apprehension. In 1771 he engaged William Crawford to survey for him a 587-acre tract of prime bottom land here.

At the southern end of Round Bottom the highway pressed close to the river for two miles in a narrows that finally opened into Cresap Bottom. Nothing quite prepared me for the sight which awaited us there. The first thing to catch our eye was three gigantic chimneys rising from the plain and disappearing into the morning clouds above. These were the smokestacks of American Electric Power Company's Kammer Station, a massive coal-fired electric-generating plant on the river. Proceeding south we then passed the smokestacks and cooling towers of Kammer's sister plant, the Mitchell Station. The two-mile-long bottom is almost entirely filled with industrial plants. We turned around and drove back to Graveyard Run, parking on the gravel shoulder at the entrance to a coal mine (**Stop 1**). Graveyard Run was the site of Baker's Fort.

About 1784, John Baker and his sons built a small blockhouse on the south side of this run at the upper end of Cresap Bottom.[68] The fort was eight miles downstream from Tomlinson's Fort at Grave Creek and three miles upstream from the mouth of Fish Creek. A later Cresap resident, Friend Cox, described the area around the old fort in 1886:

> Bakers Fort was I think situated on the river bank just south of Graveyard Run (or Bloody Run as the old settlers called it) and I think a distance of two or three hundred yards from the spring. There is no second bank here and from this run north for three miles the bottom is

Background and Overview

very narrow and is known as the narrows. The springs is on the north side of the run and issues or boils up from the base of the mountain, or hill, as we call it. The hill is very steep from there to the summit, with several ledges of rock jutting out. Its height is three hundred feet I think. There is a very large depression around the spring. Some term it a bear wallow and the water use to stand in this depression about one foot deep, very clear and pretty, but now the railroad has trestled right through this and dams up the spring and nearly spoils it.[69]

The graveyard nestled in a grove of trees behind Baker's Fort was the burial place of the Rangers killed in the battle of Captina. Captain John Baker, who built the fort, as well as John Wetzel, Indian fighter and patriarch of the Wetzel clan in Ohio County, were also buried there.[70]

My wife stayed in the car reading while I headed off to look for Baker's Fort and the old cemetery. I climbed over the guardrail at the edge of the highway and down a bank, then over the railroad tracks and down another bank to Graveyard Run. The run was bone dry. Its rocky bed emerges from a culvert running under the railroad and cuts through the woods and undergrowth to the river, less than one hundred yards in all. In the area south of the run stands a massive coal preparation plant. The plant had been built on fill in order to keep it out of the flood plain. Fill—boiler slag and clinkers—also covered the spot where the graveyard should have been.

I walked over to the plant to see if anybody was around to talk to and met a couple of friendly workers—Stacy and Sherman Knox. Stacy filled me in on the history of the coal preparation plant. It had been built by Hanna Coal Company to clean the coal taken out of their Ireland mine and load it onto barges at the river port. Coal is shipped from Marshall County to power plants up and down the Ohio River. The Ireland mine is now closed and the prep plant is no longer cleaning coal. The facility is owned by Consolidated Coal Company, which operates the McElroy mine and preparation plant, located just to the south of Ireland. The coal cleaned at McElroy is conveyed north about a mile—surprisingly, bypassing the two power plants—to Ireland, which still has a barge-loading facility. Stacy Knox was familiar with the old pioneer cemetery and thought that it had been moved when the Ireland prep plant was built. It is difficult to determine precisely where Baker's Fort stood. If the fort was close to the river bank, as reported, the site could lie under water; because of the dams, the Ohio River is now a much wider stream than it once was. If not under water, then the fort site is probably buried under fill.

We continued south on Route 2. This bottom was named for Michael Cresap, one of the early land speculators in the area.[71] His son, Michael Cresap, Jr., later settled in the bottom named for his father. Michael, Jr., was living there when another tourist, Fortescue Cumings, passed through in 1808 on a trip down the Ohio River:

> We passed Captina creek on the right, emptying into the Ohio through an extensive bottom, with three mills and several settlements on it. A mile lower, on the left is Baker's station, which has the appearance of an old settlement. About three miles below Captina creek we stopped on the left at Mr. Cressop's fine farm. He was on the plantation overseeing his labourers, but Mrs. Cressop received us politely. She is young and very handsome, and her employments of rocking her infant in its cradle while she exercised her needle, did not diminish any thing of her beauty or respectability.... Mr. Cressop owns a thousand acres of land here in one body, most of it first rate bottom, his cottage is well furnished, and he has a neat and good garden.[72]

We crossed the bridge over Fish Creek and took a little gravel road out to a boat landing near the point (**Stop 2**, see accompanying map). Another visitor, who stopped at Fish Creek in 1803, saw this area as it was and as it might become. Thaddeus Harris's unsentimental vision of the future Cresap Bottom has now come true:

> Here fine cultivated plains and rising settlements charm the eye amidst the boundless prospect of desolate wilds. When we see the land cleared of those enormous trees with which it was overgrown, and the cliffs and quarries converted into materials for building, we cannot help dwelling upon the industry and art of man, which by dint of toil and perseverance can change the desert into a fruitful field, and shape the rough rock to use and elegance. When the solitary waste is peopled, and convenient habitations arise amidst the former retreats of wild beasts; when the silence of nature is succeeded by the buzz of employment, the congratulations of society, and the voice of joy; in fine, when we behold competence and plenty springing from the bosom of dreary forests,—what a lesson is afforded of the benevolent intentions of Providence![73]

After the forest was cleared by the original settlers, the next signal of progress in Cresap Bottom was the coming of the railroad. Besides the visible—not to mention audible—changes it brought to the bottom, the Ohio River Railroad (now Conrail) added an essential ingredient for industrial growth. Still, the area was mostly farmland until the 1940s. There was a small village at Cresap built around the Cresap coal mine, which went out of business during the Great Depression. The WPA paved Route 2 and built a new bridge over Fish Creek. With the resurgence of coal demand during and after World War II, industry began locating all along the bottom. The Kammer electric plant's first unit went in in 1958; the Ireland mine opened in 1956 on Hog Run; and the McElroy mine and Mitchell electric plant opened in 1970. Since that time, these and other mineral industries have expanded to fill the bottom, driving out all signs of farm and village.

Parked off the highway, out of sight and sound of modern industry, we watched a blue heron fishing near the creek bank.

This scene, at least, was little changed since pioneer times. We tried to picture the point as Cumings saw it, when he stopped in 1808:

> We passed [Robert] Woods's fine island, about a mile long, and stopped just beyond it at Biddle's tavern on the left, at the conflux of Fish creek and the Ohio, a mile and a half below [Michael] Cressop's. Biddle keeps a ferry over Fish creek, which is a fine deep stream, fifty yards wide, running thirty miles through the country, but having no mills on it yet.... Biddle has ten acres of corn on the island, which contains fifty acres of the first quality of soil above the highest flood marks, the rest being liable to inundation.[74]

We turned around and headed back up Route 2. At the southern end of the bottom near Fish Creek, the land to the east is dotted with low hills, but the hills become higher and steeper on the northern end approaching the narrows. The river elevation at normal pool is 610 feet above sea level; the hills near the narrows rise to about 1100 feet.[75]

As we passed Graveyard Run, we could see our next destination across the river—Powhatan Point. To get there, we had to backtrack to Moundsville. We ate lunch at Blake's on Lafayette Avenue, made a quick stop at the library on Fifth Street, then drove across the new bridge to Belmont County, Ohio. Route 7 took us into Powhatan Point. Just before the railroad underpass in town, we turned right onto Cove Road, which runs parallel to Captina Creek. We drove half a mile up Cove Road to where a gravel road intersects on the right, and we parked there (**Stop 3**).

Running beside the gravel road, on the east side, was what looked like a drainage ditch, but shows up on the topo map as an intermittent stream. This is Cove Run, from which the road takes its name. The area fits the general description of the battle site provided in several of the Captina accounts (see McDonald, Tomlinson and Hollister in Part III). The "prairie," the "Indian field" and the "cove" mentioned in these accounts must refer to the plain in the bend of Captina, most of it lying on the south side of the creek and now part of the Clair Mar Golf Course on Route 148. There are two places we saw that would have made good ambush sites. One was the hill due east of where we were parked; it overlooks Cove Run and would have offered good fields of fire. Another spot was due south of the intersection, near where Cove Run empties into Captina Creek; there is a narrow bottom (perhaps fifty to seventy-five yards wide) on the north side of the creek, and the embankment above would have been a good spot to fire down on Rangers walking up the creek. Building the railroad and the road and mining activity has probably altered the landscape dramatically since the time of the Captina affair. Even though the terrain may be different now, I felt we had to be very close to the battle site. Fixing the location any more precisely may not be possible today.

We went up Cove Road a few hundred yards farther and stopped at the home of Rick Hess. Rick was in the front yard directing a roofing project but took time out to visit with us. He was familiar with the battle and much of the Indian lore of Captina; knew where Indian graves had been dug into on several nearby hills; and had heard of countless artifacts being found along the creek. Rick did not know exactly where the battle of Captina took place and did not think that anyone else in Powhatan knew either. His house on the south side of Cove Road overlooks the creek; the bank behind the house descends steeply to the water. Here in the bend, the creek is wide and still, being in the backwater of the Ohio. There is a scenic view in all directions. Looking south over the hills beyond Captina Creek, I saw the top of a smokestack, a reminder that Baker's Fort was not far off.

We then traveled down to the Point, the confluence of Captina with the Ohio **(Stop 4)**. This is a beautiful spot, quiet and shaded by old trees. Here, with the urban and industrial development largely blocked from view, one can picture the area as it was two hundred years ago. While at Captina in 1770, George Washington made the following entries in his journal:

> [October 24] Two or three Miles below the Pipe Creek is a pretty large Creek on the West side called by [Joseph] Nicholson Fox-Grape Vine, by others Captema Creek, on which, eight Miles up it, is the Town called the Grape Vine Town; and at the Mouth of it, is the place where it was said the Traders lived, and the one was killed. To this place we came about three Oclock in the Afternoon, and finding no body there, we agreed to Camp....
>
> [October 25] About half an hour after seven we set out from our Incampment around which, and up the Creek is a body of fine Land. In our Passage down to this, we see innumerable quantities of Turkeys, and many Deer watering, and brousing on the Shore side, some of which we killed. Neither yesterday nor the day before did we pass any Rifts or very rapid water—the River gliding gently along—nor did we perceive any alteration in the general face of the Country, except that the bottoms seemed to be getting a little longer and wider, as the Bends of the River grew larger.[76]

Captina Creek was once well known for the grape vines that grew along its banks, as well as for the old village called "Grape Vine Town," located on the creek a few miles west of Powhatan Point.[77]

Our next stop was on Main Street at the home of Victor and Carolyn Rutter, whom we were told had a wealth of knowledge on Powhatan Point. Victor teaches history at Ohio University and participates in an annual reenactment of George Washington's landing at Captina. Carolyn has nearly completed a history of the town and will be publishing soon. She spread out some of her materials on the parlor floor, and we spent an hour talking about Powhatan Point, old and new.

This area of York Township was first settled near the close of the eighteenth century; the township was established in 1801. By

Background and Overview

the time the town was surveyed by Dr. DeHass in 1849, there were already a number of houses standing along the river. Named after a famous Indian chief of Virginia, the town developed slowly and suffered through periodic flooding of the Ohio River, the worst in 1936. In 1922, North American Coal Company opened the first Powhatan mine; six more would follow. Coal mining ushered in an era of growth and prosperity, occasionally interrupted by disaster, such as the 1944 fire that killed sixty-six miners. During a wave of consolidation "improvements" in 1969, the high school at Powhatan was closed, which was a blow to civic pride and unity. Most of the coal mines have shut down—victim of federal regulations to limit the use of high-sulfur coal—and the community is going through a phase of economic readjustment.

Taking leave of the Rutter's, we drove down Route 7 and pulled off where the road again comes close to the river, south of Powhatan (**Stop 5**). Here the railroad runs between the highway and the river, and one can look across the water to the hollow where Graveyard Run cuts through the hills. The features that most readily stand out at that distance, however, are the immense coal silos. After seeing the lay of the land, it is tempting to speculate on the Rangers' route to the battle site. When the company crossed the river from Baker's Fort, they would have landed near this place, south of town. They probably took a path to Captina roughly parallel to the present highway. Upon intersecting the creek, they must have gone upstream for a ways along the south bank, as a steep hill runs along the north shore. After passing the hill, the Rangers no doubt crossed Captina to the north shore and proceeded but a short distance to the site where the ambush took place.

Having begun the day at dawn, my wife and I returned to Wheeling at dusk. We crossed the Old Suspension Bridge to Wheeling Island and treated ourselves to a steak dinner at Abbey's. We recrossed the bridge and closed the day by driving down Main Street past the site of old Fort Henry. Sadly, this famed historic fort is no longer highlighted in local tourist guides.⁷⁸

As a footnote to the trip, I have since learned the fate of the pioneer cemetery at Baker's Fort. This information comes from Naomi Lowe of the Marshall County Historical Society. When the industrial site was being constructed at Cresap Bottom, the markers in the old graveyard were moved to a new location—the Americana Roadside Park—just across Route 2. (In *Belmont County History* there is a photograph of Raymond and Ross Baker in the park, standing beside the monument of Captain John Baker.⁷⁹) A few years ago, when Route 2 was widened, the roadside park was closed and the markers were moved again: John Baker's to Riverview Cemetery on Round Bottom Hill, and John Wetzel's to a cemetery on McCreary Ridge, east of Moundsville. These moves involved only markers and stones; no bodies were found when the cemetery behind the fort was relocated.⁸⁰ Undoubtedly, the pioneer remains are still at rest under the slag heaps beside Graveyard Run.

PART II

AN INQUIRY INTO THE CAPTINA AFFAIR

Analysis

Before discussing the battle itself, it may be worthwhile to present a brief analysis of the sources that are available on Captina, which are identified below by the name of the person who wrote or otherwise left the record:

Martin Baker	John McDonald
Daniel Bain	George McKiernan
John Bain	David Shepherd
Ezekiel Boggs	John Shoptaw
John Dailey	Samuel Tomlinson
Wills de Hass	Daniel Wire
William Harrod, Jr.	John Yoho
Samuel Hedges	York [Pa.] *General-Advertiser*
Jeremiah Hollister	

Sources include a newspaper article, letters, interviews, depositions, a biography, pension applications and several published narratives. These accounts, left over a period of seventy years, are reprinted in their entirety in Part III. They are interesting to study from the aspect of how the telling of a tale evolves in the retelling over a period of many years. In some instances the records present seemingly contradictory descriptions of the same events. Over a century ago, Lyman Draper wrote to the author (Jeremiah Hollister) of one of the narratives and questioned him sharply concerning a number of discrepancies in his account. Hollister's version, however, was by then a set-piece, and he could shed little light on the issues Draper raised.[81] I should mention that at this time it is still not possible to reconcile all the different versions of Captina.

In order to assess reliability, each account was examined, compared to the others and evaluated in light of available historical material. It may be appropriate to give a brief critique here. Other things being equal, when relying on a person's memory of events, one would expect that accounts set down soon after the events occurred would be more accurate than those written later. With the exception of the two contemporary reports, the earliest accounts of Captina were written more than forty years after the battle. These accounts may be dated as follows (in parenthesis): John Bain, John Dailey, John Shoptaw and John Yoho (1832), Daniel Bain (1833), John McDonald (1838), Abelard Tomlinson and George McKiernan (1843), William Harrod, Jr. (1845), Martin Baker (1846), Wills de Hass (1851), Ezekiel Boggs (1855-59), Jeremiah Hollister (1862) and Samuel Hedges (1863). One would generally regard first-hand accounts more highly than accounts relying on second- or third-hand information. Eyewitness reporters on Captina include Baker, the Bains, Dailey, Shoptaw, McArthur and Yoho. (Dailey's and Yoho's accounts refer to a second, later event at Baker's Fort in 1791, as will be shown below.) McArthur's story was told by his biographer and brother-in-law, John McDonald. Others who were personally acquainted with participants include Boggs, Harrod, Hedges, Hollister and Tomlinson. The accounts of McKiernan and de Hass are the most derivative and may be composites of various versions of events. In fact, de Hass "borrows" to a degree from McKiernan, as indicated by a number of similarly worded passages.

In the analysis that follows, repeated footnotes to source materials are omitted, since the complete sources follow in Part III. Spelling of names—not a matter of great importance in the eighteenth century—varied widely in all accounts of the battle. A consistent spelling has been used in this report, except in quoted material where spelling follows the original.

The first question that arises concerning the Captina affair is when did the battle occur? Accounts vary, placing the year from 1791 to 1794, and the time of year from spring to early summer. Of those who supplied dates, de Hass, Hollister, McKiernan and Shoptaw reported that Captina occurred in 1791; McDonald in

An Inquiry into the Captina Affair

1792; Harrod in 1793; and Baker in 1794. When testimony about an event conflicts, resolution is best obtained from original documents prepared nearly contemporaneously with the event. Fortunately, two such documents exist—Colonel David Shepherd's letter to Secretary of War Henry Knox and a newspaper article in the *York General-Advertiser*. Written on May 6, 1791, Shepherd's dispatch pinpoints the time—"within a few days past"—and mentions the death of Ensign Enox and the wounding of Ensign Biggs, referring to the Captina and Kirkwood affairs, respectively. The letter is in Shepherd's own hand. The original document is preserved at the Wisconsin State Historical Society and is reproduced in the microfilm collection of Lyman C. Draper's manuscripts (in the "Shepherd Papers"). Shepherd's dispatch makes it unnecessary to have to choose between the conflicting dates which were put forth decades after the event. The second piece of evidence—the newspaper article published on May 25, 1791—gives the dates for the actions at Kirkwood's and Captina as April 30 and May 1, respectively. The article also places the Crow family incident in the same timeframe.

Drawing on all of the available sources, we can begin to piece together the sequence of events that led up to the battle. Most important in this regard is William Harrod, Jr.'s interview. Harrod, who lived near present-day Jefferson, Greene County, should be a reliable informant as he was the near neighbor of a number of the Rangers who were at Captina. Harrod himself was on duty with the militia at that time. A pay roll indicates that he received $3.90 for service as a private from April 16 to May 24, 1791.[82] Although Harrod mistakenly gave the year as 1793, his account confirms the proximity of the Crow family massacre and the Captina affair. Harrod could have been mistaken about the year or Lyman Draper, his interviewer, may have miscopied it.

The Crow sisters were killed on Sunday, May 1, 1791, on the Dunkard fork of Wheeling. Three miles up Dunkard fork from the massacre site was a Ranger outpost on the land of Thomas

Ryerson[83] that was known as Ryerson's Station or Ryerson's Blockhouse. Harrod stated that at that time his father, William Harrod, Sr., "commanded a blockhouse high up on Wheeling Creek, some twenty-two miles." The only blockhouse fitting this precise description is Ryerson's Station. It is likely that the first alarm of the massacre would have been delivered there. The Crow massacre is the only event William, Jr., refers to during his father's tenure at Ryerson's:

> While Harrod was at the blockhouse up Wheeling in spring of 1793, perhaps in May, Captain William Enochs with a party of men pursued Indians that had killed two of the widow Crow's daughters.[84]

William Enoch may have been at Ryerson's Station that day, or Harrod may have sent word to him at Fort Enoch, which was located about five miles northeast of Ryerson's. This fort—also referred to as Gray's Station or Enoch's Station—was used as a Ranger base in conjunction with Ryerson's in 1791-94.[85]

William Harrod, Sr., may have ordered the Rangers out on their mission after receiving the alarm from the Crow's. This is implied by his son's statement that "Harrod had cautioned Captain Enochs not to follow much over the river." Harrod and Enoch must have discussed the operation, at least, for Harrod to have issued a warning about pursuing beyond the Ohio River. Whatever the exchange, it seems reasonable for the twenty-nine-year-old Enoch to have headed the mission rather than Harrod, who was about fifty-four years old at the time.

Since Ryerson's blockhouse was only three miles from the massacre site, word of that morning's tragedy certainly would have reached the company there by the afternoon of May 1. Assuming the Rangers left the same afternoon, they could easily have covered the seventeen miles to Baker's Fort in a few hours if they were mounted. There is no evidence to indicate if they were mounted or not, but even on foot, they could have made it to Baker's in five or six hours, getting there by Sunday night.

Indians and Rangers may have used branches of the Warrior Trail to reach the Ohio River. Native Americans had long used this east-west path to go to and from the Ohio country. Crossing the river just north of Fish Creek, the trail follows a series of ridges that ultimately stretch all the way to the Monongahela River, near Greensboro in Greene County. After striking the trail south of Ryerson's, the Rangers would have come to the river just south of Baker's Fort.[86]

Pairing Harrod's account with Colonel Shepherd's dispatch and the newspaper article, we can reconstruct the following chain of events. On Sunday morning, May 1, the Crow sisters were killed by three Indians on the Dunkard fork of Wheeling Creek. Presumably, the Indians beat a retreat west, crossing the Ohio River somewhere between Baker's Fort and the mouth of Grave Creek. Word reached Ryerson's Station that afternoon, and a detachment of Rangers under the command of William Enoch went in pursuit of the Indians. By Sunday night, the Rangers had reached Baker's Fort.

There were two engagements with Indians that occurred near Baker's Fort during the Captina affair. The first was an incident, in which a party of scouts on the Ohio side of the river was fired upon by Indians, resulting in several casualties. The second was a battle that took place during a follow up action to the first, in which the company sent over in pursuit of the Indians was ambushed on Captina Creek and suffered additional casualties. Several accounts placed these events on the same day, but the weight of evidence indicates that they occurred on consecutive days. The scouting mission will be referred to from here on as the "first day" and the ambush on Captina as the "second day."

Given that the Crow sisters were killed the morning of May 1 and the Rangers probably arrived at Baker's Fort that afternoon or evening, it seems reasonable to assume that the events of the first day took place on May 1 as stated in the newspaper account. Martin Baker stated that four scouts—John Daniels, Adam

Miller, Isaac McCowan and John Shoptaw—were sent over that day, "according to the custom, to the Ohio side to reconnoitre." John Shoptaw stated in his pension application that he enlisted in Henry Enoch's company on March 1 and that the county lieutenant, James Marshel, appointed Shoptaw to lead a detachment of scouts composed of himself, Daniels, Miller and McCowan. De Hass and Tomlinson added John Bain to the list of scouts. John Bain was present on the second day, and he was involved in another incident while "scouting" at Captina Creek in June of 1791. It seems probable that these two incidents, when recalled years later, were mistakenly combined.

Eleven-year-old Martin Baker was at the fort, and that day's events left a vivid impression upon him. In later years he was fond of telling his version of Captina. One of his neighbors, Jeremiah Hollister, recalled, "I have often heard Martin Baker relate the account of the Battel." According to Baker's version, four scouts were sent over to the Ohio side to reconnoiter:

> They were Adam Miller, John Daniels, Isaac McCowan, and John Shoptaw. Miller and Daniels took up stream, and the other two down. The upper scouts were soon attacked by Indians, and Miller killed; Daniels ran up Captina about three miles, but being weak from the loss of blood issuing from a wound in his arm, was taken prisoner [and] carried into captivity.

Baker stated that Daniels was released at the treaty of Greenville in 1795.

Upon hearing the guns, the other group of scouts ran for their canoes. Before they made it, the Indians fired on them, too. The whites then ran down river and reached a point nearly opposite the fort with the Indians still in pursuit. There they shot Isaac McCowan on the sandy bank of the river. John Shoptaw jumped into the Ohio and began to swim across. The Indians showed themselves on the bank, where they scalped McCowan and fired on Shoptaw. Shoptaw made it to the Virginia side alive.

An Inquiry into the Captina Affair

One more noteworthy incident that day was later reported. According to Jeremiah Hollister,

> The Indians made their appearance opesite the fort and, being able to speak some Englis, hallowed over to the fort, repeating several times, "Turn out, turn out."

Hollister, though not present at the Captina affair, was personally acquainted with men who were—Daniel and John Bain, Martin Baker and John Daniels. Several other accounts make mention of the fact that a few Indians showed themselves across the river on the first day. At this point the Rangers were not aware of the presence of a larger body of Indians.

Duncan McArthur, one of the key figures on the second day, does not mention any of the events of the first day, indicating that he was not present during the incident but, rather, was with the Rangers pursuing from Ryerson's Station. This suggests that the scouts were at the fort and had already been fired upon and returned before the party of men arrived from Ryerson's. The Rangers got to the fort and made camp along the river. According to McDonald, McArthur's biographer,

> Shortly after their encamping on the river, and at a late hour in the evening, a few Indians were discovered across the river from the fort, on the Ohio shore, carelessly walking about.

McArthur expressed the opinion that the Indians purposely showed themselves to invite pursuit. It is not clear that he was aware of this fact at the time.

Several of the Captina accounts suggest that after the scouts were fired on the Rangers went in pursuit of the Indians almost at once. McKiernan, for example, wrote that as soon as Shoptaw related his story:

> All the able-bodied men at the post—sixteen in number—promptly volunteered for the service; and, without loss of time, marched up the bank, and crossed over opposite the mouth of Captina.

To McKiernan this may have seemed consistent with the Rangers' reputation for courage and boldness. Tomlinson, however, wrote that *"preparation* was immediately made to go in pursuit of the Indians" and that may be more accurate. Hollister wrote that "the next morning the men, seventeen in number, left the station to fight the Indians." Lyman Draper worried about this question clear back in 1862 and wrote to Hollister that

> It would be difficult to judge from the several narratives, whether the four spies went over the same day of the fight, or the night before.[87]

I believe McArthur—as the only participant to address the issue—should be taken as the authority on this point. He stated that, following the arrival of the company and the discovery of the Indians across the river, the men started out in pursuit "early the next morning."

Immediate pursuit following the incident with the scouts may not have been practical with the contingent of Rangers at the fort at that time. It is uncertain how many men were present there in addition to the scouts, but the number had been reduced by three that morning with the loss of Daniels, Miller and McCowan (or by four, if Shoptaw was wounded). Whatever the reason, the mission appears to have been delayed until the following morning.

In those days military commanders frequently called for a "council of war" after an engagement in order to plan the next movement. The authority of militia leaders was fairly loose, by today's standards, and in some ways discipline was loose, too. Officers tended to lead by building consensus, and those who were better at getting agreement tended to be better officers. A man might be elected to head his company simply because he possessed that ability. Officers were expected to consult with any man who had an opinion when planning what strategy to pursue. Such a council of war likely followed the killing of the scouts on May 1.

We can postulate some of the issues that would have been raised. Those favoring immediate pursuit would have suggested that any hesitation might allow the Indians time to get away and escape retaliation. Or they may have argued that delaying pursuit would permit the few Indians present to be reinforced. Those favoring delay would have pointed out that the Indians may have been feigning small numbers, attempting to draw the Rangers into an ambush—a favorite tactic of the Indians. This side may have argued that it would be prudent to delay the mission until reinforcements arrived from Ryerson's. The York County newspaper article stated that

> The party of rangers [at Baker's Fort] were waiting for information from Lieutenant Enix, who commanded the party on Dunkard Creek. . . .

It is quite possible that they were waiting on more Rangers rather than "information."

Martin Baker suggests another element that may have been introduced into the council of war. He states that there seemed to be "much reluctance among them to volunteer" and that his sister[88] was moved to exclaim that "she wouldn't be a coward." That word—coward—had almost magical properties then. Even when used by the foolish to propose some rash act, the word could cause men of sounder judgment to abandon their position for fear of being branded cowards. There may not have been a more loathsome characteristic among the pioneers; cowards were at the bottom of the social scale.[89] One of the worst defeats suffered by militia troops on the early frontier, the battle of Blue Licks in Kentucky, is alleged to have been caused by the "C-word." After Bryan's Station was captured in 1782, the militia organized a pursuit and was soon hot on the trail of the retreating Wyandot. The force was commanded by colonels John Todd, Stephen Trigg and Daniel Boone. When this army came upon the heels of the Indians at Blue Licks, a council was called. Boone said it appeared that the Indians had allowed themselves to be "caught" and suggested waiting on the reinforcements of Colonel Benjamin Logan, who was not far behind. The others agreed. According to legend, Hugh McGary then uttered his famous remark: "Let all who are not cowards follow me." All followed, including Boone, and the Wyandot were waiting for them. In a matter of minutes, nearly seventy of the 180-man force were killed and many more wounded or captured. Among the dead were Todd, Trigg and Daniel Boone's son Israel.

Returning to Captina and the council of war at Baker's Fort, it appears that cooler heads prevailed. There was no rash pursuit as happened at Blue Licks. The party at Baker's was reinforced by the evening of May 1, and a plan for pursuit was implemented the following morning. According to Duncan McArthur, a party under Abraham Enoch[90] crossed the river before daylight and proceeded to where the Indians had fired on the scouts from the bank. The names of those reported to have been out with Abraham Enoch on the second day include John Baker, Daniel Bain, John Bain, Alexander Boggs, John Line, Duncan McArthur, George McColloch, Abraham McCowan, John Sutherland, Ray Vennam, Dobbins, Hoffman and Downing. This list of fourteen men may be a few short of the actual number. The number reported to have been in the company varied in the accounts, ranging from fourteen to twenty. Others who may have been present at Baker's Fort and who could have been in the company include Joseph Baker and Henry Baker (brothers of John), John Dailey, John Yoho and a man named Tate.

At first light on May 2, the Rangers started upstream and easily found the Indians' trail, which soon became distinct, if not obvious. The accounts vary to some degree regarding the route

An Inquiry into the Captina Affair

taken to Captina and the location of the battle site. McArthur is the only participant who gives the route to Captina, and his account is given preference below. Hollister later visited the battlefield with several participants, so he is accorded primacy on that point. (See the accompanying sketch maps.)

According to McArthur's biography,

> Early the next morning Lieutenant Enoch with fifteen men, amongst whom was McArthur, crossed the river before day. As soon as it was light enough to distinguish objects at a distance, Lieutenant Enoch and his party went to the place where the Indians had showed themselves the previous evening, and found the trail of five or six Indians, and incautiously pursued them over the river hill to Captina creek.

"The river hill" refers to the bank across the Ohio River from Baker's Fort. The bank today rises thirty feet above the river level and would have been even higher prior to the Ohio River being raised behind a series of locks and dams. From the river the Rangers probably proceeded to the northeast, skirting a high hill on their left, until they struck Captina Creek. McArthur said they intercepted the creek "about one mile from the river, and not much further from the mouth of the creek."[91] The signs up to this time still indicated that they were following a small group of Indians. The Rangers advanced along the creek bottom in single file. The creek at this point curves to the north and several small streams empty into Captina from the north side. Tomlinson called the area "an Indian field, or prairie." Judge Hollister was shown the site by Daniel Bain in 1809. Hollister said the place was "known as the cove," and he made a drawing for Lyman Draper showing the location of the cove on Captina. The area still goes by that name, and the road paralleling the creek there is called Cove Road.[92]

Whatever plan the Rangers had that day was foiled by the Indians—a Shawnee war party led by a chief named Charley Wilkey. Showing only a few Indians the day before and leaving an obvious trail for the Rangers to follow was part of a trap set by the Shawnee. Hollister stated that the Rangers followed the trail up Captina on the south side of the creek. Near the cove the trail crossed the creek and headed a little north, striking one of the small runs. Hollister described the setting:

> Two small runs or dreans come in to the creek [Captina] two or three hundred yards apart and between these runs there is a low ridge where our men were led into ambush.

Enoch's party stayed on the trail, following the little stream. The tracks continued along the run through a low area flanked by rising ground. The Indians were strung out along a heavily-wooded hillside, concealed and waiting patiently. According to McKiernan, the Indians hid behind "a bunch of dogwood trees covered with grape vines." McDonald describes how Duncan McArthur recalled the scene:

> As the party of whites were pursuing the trail, they went down a small drain, with a narrow bottom. On the right of the drain was a steep, rocky bank, fifty or sixty feet high; on this bank thirty or forty Indians lay concealed.

The Shawnee undoubtedly had scouts out that morning, and they were prepared for the Rangers' arrival. When the company entered the ambush zone in single file, the Shawnee sprang the trap, opening fire on the column from the ridge above. Amazingly, no one was killed in the first fire. The noise of thirty or forty rifles must have been deafening in the narrow ravine, and it is difficult to imagine the terror of being strung out in the open and fired upon by a well-concealed adversary. To make it worse, the Rangers were outnumbered and had no good ground to fight from. They made the best of the situation, however, quickly finding cover and returning fire. According to McDonald, the Rangers

> took shelter behind trees, logs, or rocks, and the battle was continued with animation on both sides for some

Governor Duncan McArthur
Courtesy of Ohio Historical Society, Columbus, Ohio

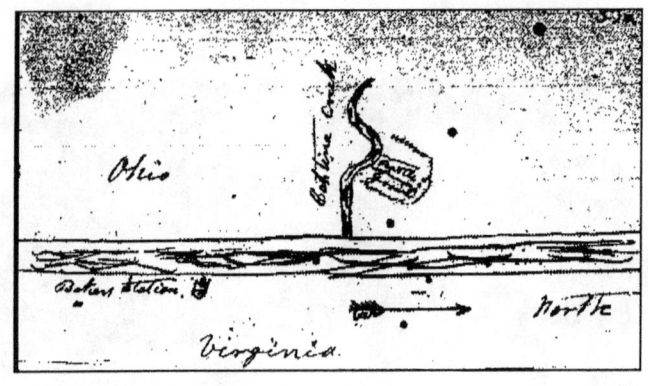

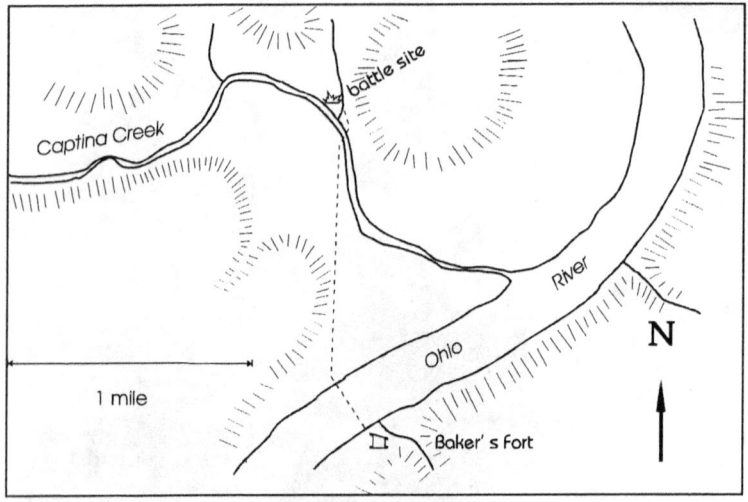

**Site of the Battleground on Captina Creek
May 2, 1791**

Legend: Top—Jeremiah Hollister's drawing of the battleground that he made for Lyman Draper (Draper 7E30). **Bottom**—Scale drawing of the area made from a topographic map showing the probable path the of Rangers on the morning of May 2, as described in Duncan McArthur's biography (John McDonald, *Biographical Sketches of General Nathaniel Massie, General Duncan McArthur, et al.*).

time. Lieutenant Enoch and McArthur were treed near each other, and loaded and shot several times.

Since McArthur was the only combatant to give a detailed account this action, it is appropriate to continue with his biography:

> The hills along Captina creek are steep, high, and craggy, the valleys narrow, so that the keen crack of the rifles, added to the deafening shouts of the combatants, causing the echo to vibrate from hill to hill, made it seem that those engaged in this strife of arms were fourfold the actual number. At length a ball from an Indian's rifle pierced the breast of the brave Lieutenant Enoch; he fell, and immediately expired.... Their commander being killed, and many of their gallant little band being slain or disabled, the remainder determined upon a retreat.

McKiernan stated that Enoch ordered a charge on the Indians' position but was killed only moments later, and the charge was not made. At that point, the Indians

> rushed out with a loud yell, brandishing their tomahawks above their heads. At the same instant, a second party of Indians, stationed about forty paces down the river, under cover of a thicket, opened a fire, which killed John Baker and a man named Hoffman, besides wounding three others.

John Baker was not killed during this fire but may have been wounded. Martin Baker also referred to a second body of Indians, stating that they came up behind and shot Enoch and Hoffman.

De Hass implies that McArthur attempted to lead a charge on the Indians, writing that "young McArthur cried out, as they ascended the bank, to 'surround them.'" While this action is not corroborated, several accounts do credit McArthur with rising to the occasion and leading the company after their commander was killed. McArthur himself said so, according to McDonald:

> No officer was left to command, and although McArthur was the youngest man in the company, in this time of peril he was unanimously called to direct the retreat.

Hollister presented an "honorable" explanation for the ensuing retreat:

> It was proposed by some of our men to run a few rods back up a hill, there being a thick cluster of small beach [beech] in the way between them and the enemy. They by so doing could shoot over the beach bushes. When the other men who had not heard the conversation seen them run, [they] supposed it to be a retreat and run also, and the panict became general and they could not be checked.

While something like this could have occurred, the retreat was undoubtedly necessitated by the heavy losses the Rangers had sustained at that point. It is likely that half their number was by then dead or wounded.

The Shawnee pressed their attack on the retreating Rangers and were able to inflict a few more casualties. John Baker was shot during the withdrawal. Downing stopped to assist, but Baker's wounds were too serious and he could not go on. Martin Baker described his brother John's fate:

> On [the] retreat my brother was shot in the hip. Determined to sell his life as dearly as possible, he drew off [to] one side and secreted himself in a hollow with a rock at his back, offering no chance for the enemy to approach but in front. Shortly after, two guns were heard in quick succession; doubtless one of them was fired by my brother, and from the signs afterwards, it was supposed he had killed an Indian.

George McColloch either got shot in the ankle (de Hass) or sprained his ankle (Tomlinson) and could not keep up with the company. De Hass said that one of the Rangers came to McColloch's aid:

> Ray Vennam . . . took him on his shoulder and carried him some distance, but McColloch, finding that they would be overtaken, entreated the other to take care of himself. Vennam concealed McColloch behind a log, and made his way to the fort.

Later, under the cover of darkness, McColloch was able to make his way back to the river. Accounts differ on how he got back to the fort. Tomlinson said McColloch arrived at the Grave Creek blockhouse "about ten o'clock the next day." De Hass describes a daring rescue of McColloch during the night:

> That night a man's plaintive cry was heard from the opposite shore, and on Vennam saying it was George McColloch, those in the fort said no, it was an Indian. Vennam, however, was firm in his opinion that it was his friend, and accordingly went over in a canoe to get McColloch.

The idea raised earlier about a "second body" of Indians is indirectly supported by the fact that most of the men made their way to Tomlinson's Fort rather than Baker's Fort. If the Rangers had retreated downstream along Captina, Baker's would have been the closer fort. From the mouth of Captina on the Ohio River, it was one mile south to Baker's and seven miles north to Grave Creek. It is possible that at the battleground the route along Captina was blocked by the "second body," requiring the men to head north over land. If the Rangers' retreat took a northern route, they would have had to pass through some rugged terrain before striking the Ohio River about three miles west of Grave Creek.

While we have a number of accounts of Captina from the whites' perspective, scant information is available on the battle

Affair at Captina Creek

from the Shawnee's point of view. The captive, John Daniels, was with the Indians on the day of the battle. Hollister wrote that Daniels returned to Baker's Fort after his release from captivity and "related his story." Daniels confirmed that the Shawnee were expecting a fight that morning and were prepared for the Rangers. Hollister gave this account:

> The spy John Daniels, who had been taken prisenor the day before, was tied to a dogwood saplin on top of the hill, and one indian left with him with orders, if the indians were whiped, for the indian to tomahawk Daniels and run. If not, to loose him and join the company.

After defeating the Rangers and driving them from the field, the Shawnee pursued the retreating militia for some distance before returning to the battleground to tend to their dead and wounded, as well as to kill any surviving whites and mutilate the bodies. The Indians suffered heavy losses themselves. Some years later, after peace was made with the Indians, McDonald got to know Charley Wilkey, who had led the Shawnee at Captina. McDonald talked to Wilkey about the battle and then included the following passage in McArthur's biography:

> He [Charley Wilkey] told the author of this narrative that the battle of Captina was the most severe conflict he ever witnessed; that although he had the advantage of the ground and the first fire, he lost the most men, half of them having been either killed or wounded.

The prisoner John Daniels was the first white to view the field after the battle. He confirmed that the Shawnee had at least seven warriors killed in the action. According to Judge Hollister:

> Daniels was conducted down to the Battle ground where the indians buried or covered their dead with stone. There were seven indians killed and ware laid in a row and covered with a large pile of stone.

The Shawnee gathered their wounded and left the area. They probably proceeded on a westerly course for at least thirty miles. At that point, they pitched one of the captured weapons into a creek, where it was later recovered. Daniel Wire wrote that the gun had belonged to "Jack Bean" [i.e., John Bain] and that John Baker had borrowed it from him. The Shawnee took the gun when they killed Baker and no doubt threw it away after discovering it had gotten broken. According to Wire,

> This gun was recaptured on the waters of Wills creek, about sixteen or eighteen miles west of Woodsfield [Monroe County, Ohio], and still remains in the possession of some of the friends of the notorious Bean and the lamented Baker, in this county, as a memorial of those brave Indian fighters.

The entire action on the second day occurred in the period from before dawn until after dark. The company crossed the river before daylight, set out at first light and probably reached the cove in less than an hour—the distance being just over a mile. No one reported how long the battle lasted on the banks of Captina. McArthur provides a clue, but only in very general terms: "the battle was continued with animation on both sides for some time." He also mentions that Enoch and McArthur "loaded and shot several times" and that "at length" Enoch was killed. From that description one might estimate that the time could have been as short as ten to fifteen minutes or as long as an hour or so. The low end of that range would seem a little short for the Rangers to have killed seven concealed Indians, but beyond that one cannot be more precise. Since the battle probably ended before midmorning, the retreat must have been lengthy if, as Tomlinson stated, the Rangers did not all get to Grave Creek until that evening.

Five of the Rangers killed on May 2 are identified in the accounts on the battle. They include Abraham Enoch, John Baker, Abraham McCowan, John Line and Hoffman (whom Tomlinson calls "a Dutchman"). McArthur said that seven were killed, so two names may be missing from the list. McArthur added that "some [were] badly wounded," and McKiernan wrote that three were wounded in addition to Baker. McColloch may have been one of them; the other wounded are not named.

On Tuesday, May 3, the day after the engagement on Captina, the Rangers went back to retrieve their dead. McKiernan and de Hass state that the company consisted of a strong party from Grave Creek along with "most of the fugitives from the battle." The contingent at Grave Creek could have included William Enoch and the remainder of the Rangers from Ryerson's Station. Certainly, the "fugitives from the battle" needed reinforcement. They must have gone out in greater number than on May 2, since there was no way of knowing at that time whether or not the Indians were waiting to ambush the rescue party.

The Indians had left the area, however, and there were no wounded left to rescue, white or Indian. Although no Shawnee dead were found, there were indications that a number had been wounded. A few artifacts had been left behind; according to Tomlinson, they found "a sheaf of arrows, a bow, and a weasle skin full of red vermillion paint." The men also learned at this time how the Shawnee had set up the ambush—by walking across the open area, then doubling back to hide overlooking the trail. Tomlinson gave one description:

> It was discovered that the Indians had passed through the field to the opposite side, where they had turned short around, and marched back and secreted themselves near the edge of the woods, from whence the whites received the first fire.

The Rangers would have been looking for John Baker, whom they knew to be wounded. They discovered his body under the rock ledge where he had been killed by the Shawnee. At least one of the dead could not be found.[93] Many of the bodies had been "mutilated." Martin Baker's account gives the most graphic description:

> The next day the men turned out and visited the spot. Enochs, Hoffman and John Baker, were found dead and scalped. Enoch's bowels were torn out, his eyes and those of Hoffman screwed out with a wiping stick. The dead were wrapped in white hickory bark, and brought over to the Virginia side, and buried in their bark coffins.

According to the Oxford English Dictionary, a wiping stick is "a rod fitted with a piece of cloth for cleaning out the bore of a gun." The little cemetery where the Rangers buried their dead was located a short distance from Baker's Fort, on a stream aptly named Graveyard Run. A few years later, a traveler passing through Cresap Bottom set down the following in his journal:

> Wednesday, 20th July, 1808. Rode to Mr. Dickinson's, sixteen miles, to breakfast, crossing Fish Creek; from thence to Baker's to dinner, ten miles. A fine shower of rain today, which impeded our journey. Two miles below Baker's passed the remains of an old blockhouse near a number of graves, affording a romantic appearance, being in the middle of the woods, and the graves neatly paled in. I am told they are the graves of the militia who were posted here, and fell fighting the Indians.[94]

Few travelers passing that way today are aware of the Rangers sleeping near the little run.

There was another militia engagement with Indians near Baker's Fort that year. The primary sources for the incident are depositions by John and Daniel Bain, John Dailey and John Yoho, all of whom where present when this action occurred in late June or early July of 1791. The Bains referred to it as the incident at Baker's Fort, distinguishing it from the Captina Creek affair, which both men had been involved in earlier. In the later incident,

Indians attacked or besieged Baker's Fort. With one exception, there was no mention of militia or Indian casualties. John Dailey reported that he was on the Ohio side of the river that morning tending his corn and that he saw John Bain, who was out on a scout. A few minutes later Dailey heard gunfire and quickly returned to the fort. There he learned that Bain had been shot by the Indians and wounded in both thighs while swimming across the Ohio River. John Yoho reported that Bain was doctored by Joseph Biggs, who had himself been wounded two months earlier at Kirkwood's cabin. We may assume that the Indians found the fort too strong to attack and soon retired.

Dailey stated that he and Bain were at the fort with Captain Brock's company of Rangers. This was Captain Joseph Brock, who was referred to in a letter from Major General Richard Butler at Pittsburgh to David Shepherd at Wheeling, dated June 11, 1791:

> Sir, I am happy to inform you that the arrival of the United States troops at this post has enabled me to give protection to the frontier of your County, and to relieve the militia from further service at this time.
>
> I have for this purpose this day detached Captain Van Swearingen with his Company to take post at the mouth of Buffalo Creek, and Captain Joseph Brock with his Company to the mouth of Fish Creek. This force with other troops which are below them, will I flatter myself give security on the Ohio as far down as the great Kanhawa.
>
> You will therefore on receipt of this be pleased to discharge all the militia of your County that have been drawn out by virtue of the president of the United States directions contained in the letter of the Secretary of War dated the 10th day of March last directed to the Lieutenants of Counties, except, one Sergeant and five privates at each of the above mentioned two posts, to serve as guides to their scouting parties, and Spies to give the

alarm on the appearance of Indian War parties. These should be picked men known to be brave and active, well acquainted with the woods on the north side of the Ohio.[95]

Baker's Fort was usually referred to as being at the mouth of Fish Creek. The primary sources for this later incident at Baker's Fort are also included in Part III.

In Perspective

The engagements at Captina Creek were significant losses for the Rangers. They had at least nine killed, possibly an equal number wounded, and one captured. Following a cursory review of the affair, it might appear that the Rangers were ill advised to pursue the Indians after the attack on the scouts; that they were foolhardy to have been caught in an ambush; and that they fought poorly, then fled from the battle in disorderly fashion leaving their dead and wounded behind. These conclusions could in turn reflect badly on the performance of Ranger units, in general, and reduce the significance of their contribution during the Revolutionary War and after. Such views would not only be unfortunate, but also incorrect.

The importance of the Rangers on the frontiers of western Pennsylvania and Virginia is well documented, and no single incident can detract from their record of service through nearly thirty years of border wars. They have been often, and unfavorably, compared with "regular army" troops. The comparison is an unfair one, but it is instructive in pointing out some of the differences between the two.

Those drafted or volunteering for regular units of the U.S. Army ceased to be "civilians" and became "soldiers." They received military training and were outfitted with uniforms, weapons and other gear necessary for soldiering. They usually stayed with their units until they were discharged. Discipline in these units was usually good and the men usually fought well, well enough at least to defeat the British, who were thought at that time to have had the world's best army. Comparing the regular army to the militia is, as they say, "apples to oranges." The militia was not inferior, it was different. Knowledge about their contrasting backgrounds, resources, authority and assigned duties is key to understanding the differences between the army and militia.

The distinction begins with how one got to be in the militia, which was not by volunteer or draft. In Pennsylvania one became a member of the militia simply by being a free, white male between the ages of eighteen and fifty-three (in Virginia the ages were between eighteen and fifty).[96] This lack of selectivity differed greatly from the army, who, while not overly particular, could at least reject anyone not meeting their standards. When called to serve a term in the militia, a man did not cease to be a farmer and hunter, but rather added "Indian fighter" to his list of duties. The militiaman was the archetypal citizen-soldier. Serving short terms of a few months duration, usually in his own neighborhood, he continued clearing his land, planting and harvesting his crops, improving his home and tending to his family. In the militia he received little or no military training; he was given no uniform; and he was expected to bring his own rifle and horse, along with any other gear he needed. If he was lucky, the state may have provided enough lead, powder and bacon to supply his company. If not, he would have to provide these himself. He received little pay for his service and not infrequently volunteered for duty without pay. There were differences in the officers, too. A militia officer often had less authority than his regular army counterpart. Militia officers were not poor leaders unable to maintain discipline, and their reliance on the "consensus approach" to command was not a sign of weakness. Whereas a regular army officer could fall back on his "authority," the militia officer had to rely more on personality, intelligence, personal courage and experience in order to get his men to follow him.

Finally, Ranger companies were used in a manner distinctly different from army companies:

> Their primary function was to range up and down the vast western frontiers of the states gathering information and conducting hit and run raids when necessary to keep the enemy off balance.[97]

By patrolling the countryside, Rangers formed an early warning system for the wilderness areas. When a raid occurred, they might pursue the Indians and engage them if the numbers were favorable, but only in limited "hit and run" strikes. During times of serious Indian threats, the Rangers became defenders of the stations, blockhouses, and forts where families retreated for protection.

As they operated in small units, Rangers were not expected to engage Indians forces in battle—but they sometimes did. During the border wars they had to in order to survive. Neither the states nor the federal government met the western counties' needs for military support. Both were loath to send additional troops to the frontier, and in fairness, it would have taken an enormous army to accomplish the task. In the absence of regular troops, the frontiersman had to shoulder this responsibility in order to stay on his land and keep his family alive.

The annals of western history are replete with heroic figures—the names Boone, Brady, Kenton, Harrod, Wetzel and Zane are well known. Many of the familiar exploits of these individuals were carried out in their roles as members or leaders of militia units. Numberless other now-forgotten officers and men served in the militia with honor and distinction, demonstrating courage and resolve, energy and endurance, and selfless devotion to family and neighbors. For their efforts many suffered injury or death at the hands of their adversaries. Whereas army units were "thrown into battle" by their commanders, the Rangers would throw themselves into battle. The army private would fight to keep from being killed himself, while the Ranger fought to keep his home from being burned, his livestock from being slaughtered, and his wife and children from being slain.

Returning to the battle of Captina Creek, we may now look at the Rangers with a more realistic standard and not the same expectations we might have for an army company in the same situation. The year 1791 was a fearful time on the frontier. Harmar's defeat the previous October had set the stage. The first signs of war appeared in January, and by April Indians were massing on the Ohio River and executing daring raids on western Pennsylvania Virginia settlements. The Rangers had to remobilize quickly after several years of relative calm. New units were recruited and new officers were put into the field.[98] We know that Colonel Shepherd and others were complaining bitterly about the lack of suitable weapons, powder and lead. While the county lieutenants would have preferred to take the time to prepare and equip new units, the Rangers had to be rushed into service to deal with the emergency at hand. When the Indians struck twenty miles beyond the Ohio River, killing the Crow sisters in Washington County, every instinct of the frontier people called for immediate pursuit of the marauders. A company from Ryerson's Station set out on this quest.

The attack on the scouts at Captina on May 1 should be considered a hazard of war—scouting in particular—and not the result of poor execution. The ambush on May 2, however, is another matter. Abraham Enoch's inexperience may have been a factor in the defeat and may have contributed to the decision to pursue the Shawnee up Captina. Lack of leadership experience in this unit appears to have been general, as indicated by the fact that the youngest man in the company, Duncan McArthur, took over after their commander was killed. While the decision to pursue the Indians across the river on the second day may have been made "incautiously," as McArthur with the advantage of hindsight later suggested, it was a decision that other Ranger commanders would likely have made in similar circumstances. Other commanders may have been more experienced, but on the frontier lack of seasoning was not sufficient excuse for timidity or inaction. Enoch no doubt did what he felt a Ranger in his position was expected to do—he led his men on the mission they had come for, pursuing the Indians. Inexperience rather than lack of caution may have resulted in the failure to detect the Indians' trap at the cove on Captina. Again, it is simply one of the fortunes of war that men are sometimes pressed into situations for which they have not been adequately prepared. On the other hand, one should not fail to consider that the Rangers' defeat may have simply been due to the superior prowess of their Native American opponents.

When the ambush was sprung and the withering fire of thirty to forty rifles unleashed, the Rangers responded in exemplary fashion. They did not flee the field in panic, but rather stood their ground and returned the fire with effect. Abraham Enoch exhibited leadership during the battle and had the initiative to call for a charge on the Indians' position just before his untimely death. McArthur showed considerable presence taking control of the decimated company after the commander and a number of others were killed. There is no evidence that the retreat was ordered because of any loss of will or nerve. Indeed, by all accounts, the men displayed considerable courage under fire. The retreat was undoubtedly necessitated by the high percentage of casualties the company had taken in the battle. Similarly, there is no evidence that the men panicked on the retreat and broke into general flight. It seems likely that their return down Captina was blocked and that on the overland path through dense woods some of the men may have become separated. Even with the enemy in close pursuit, the Rangers continued to fight and Downing and Vennam were reported to have stopped to help their wounded comrades. The single Indian account of this action (albeit told through a white reporter) supports the contention that the Rangers put up a fierce battle. Charley Wilkey avowed that "although he had the advantage of the ground and the first fire, he lost the most men."

Affair at Captina Creek

While accounts of the Captina affair may be considered somewhat fragmentary, careful study of available evidence allows us to add an interesting chapter to the ongoing investigation of border warfare. It has been possible to reconstruct the major events occurring between May 1 and May 6 with some degree of confidence; only a few of the details remain in question. At the end of our analysis we may conclude that the battle of Captina was an extraordinary engagement between the Shawnee and a company of frontier militia. The contest was unusually severe. Even more unusual, both parties maintained the contact despite heavy losses.

From the point of view of the Shawnee, one might tell the tale of a war party that meticulously designed and methodically carried out a plan to draw the hated white enemy into a death trap. And though the plan was flawlessly executed, their adversaries fought back so fiercely that the outcome for a time hung in the balance. In similar instances in the past, the Indians after losing the advantage would have broken the contact. On this day, however, the Shawnee would not disappear into the forest. They fought, they maneuvered and they persevered until they drove their white enemy from the field.

Seen through the eyes of the Rangers, one finds the parallel tale of an unseasoned militia company that found itself in a desperate situation—out in the open, outnumbered two to one, and facing an enemy located on the high ground. Through combined actions of personal courage these men fought their enemy to a standoff, until finally the unit sustained so many casualties that it became impossible to hold their ground. The company then withdrew with reasonable order and without panic. The Rangers courageously returned to the battleground the next day, without knowing for certain whether the Indians had left or were waiting for them again, perhaps with reinforcements adding to their number. The Rangers brought their dead back home and buried them, and that was the end of the Captina affair.

Biographical Sketches

Revolutionary War veterans not only received government pensions, they were also immortalized in print, as well as legend, for their patriotic service. The men who served in the ensuing Indian War were not eligible for pensions under the acts passed to reward veterans of the Revolution and were little remembered by their countrymen for the sacrifices they made. Those who fought in the upper Ohio valley from 1791 to 1794 have had few to sing their praises. Many who made the ultimate sacrifice, by giving their lives, remain not only storyless but nameless as well. Thus, biographical data was sought to help portray those individuals reported to have been involved in the Captina affair of May 1791 or in the subsequent incident at Baker's Fort in June or July 1791. The brief sketches below are provided for the following men who can be identified.

JOHN BAKER, JR. (-1791) was the son of John Baker, Sr., who immigrated from Germany in 1755 and married Elizabeth Sullivan in Philadelphia in 1760. John, Sr., settled in western Pennsylvania, first on Dunkard Creek in about 1767, then near Catfish Camp (Washington) in 1781, before finally moving to Tomlinson's Fort at Grave Creek. About 1784 he built a fort at the upper end of Cresap Bottom for protection against the Indians. John served in the militia during the Revolutionary War and after, and in 1787, while in service with the Wetzels, he was killed by Indians just across the river from his fort. The men were at Baker's Fort and had seen some Indians walking around on the opposite bank. John's shot brought one down and the others fled. Baker and the Wetzels paddled a canoe across to take the scalp, but before this could be accomplished John was shot by the Indians who had been lurking behind. The Wetzels brought John back to the fort, where he died a few hours later.

John Baker reportedly had ten or eleven children: John, Jr., Henry, Joseph, Martin, Catherine, Margaret, Elizabeth, George,

Isaac, Jacob and possibly Mary. Henry was captured by Indians in 1781 but, aided by Simon Girty, was later released. Shortly thereafter Henry married one of the daughters of Stephen Parr and relocated to near Tomlinson's Fort. Catherine and Margaret were twins who married brothers, Peter and Henry Yoho. Little is known about John, Jr., beyond his role in the Captina affair. He may have been one of the elder sons, as the 1788 personal property tax return for Ohio County, "an accounting of the name of every white male tithable over twenty-one years," lists Henry and John Baker. We know that when John, Jr., set out on the mission with the Rangers, his brother Martin and one of his sisters remained behind in the fort. After the treaty was signed in 1795, many of the Bakers moved across the river to Ohio. John's mother, Elizabeth, went with them; she died years later, in 1836, and was buried near Woodsfield in Monroe County.[99]

DANIEL BAIN (c1764-1840) stated in his pension application that he was born near Winchester, Virginia, in 1763 or 1764 and came to Washington County, Pennsylvania, with his parents at an early age. Daniel served in the militia in 1781 and nearly every year thereafter until Anthony Wayne's victory in 1794. Daniel's Revolutionary War pension application lists service at various times under Rezin Virgin, Charles Craycraft and Gabriel Blakeney; during this time he was stationed at Atkinson's Fort on Tenmile, Virgin's Blockhouse on Chartiers Creek and at Ryerson's Station.[100] John Dailey and Daniel's brother, John Bain, gave supporting statements in his pension application (reproduced in Part III). So did William Jones:

> In the year 1782 being the summer of Colonel Crawford's defeat I was then enlisted under Captain Enoch at fort Jackson near ten mile in Pennsylvania. I frequently went to Atkinsons Fort where I became acquainted with Daniel Bane whom I understood was an enlisted soldier under the command of Major Cracraft. After that I saw him at

Riaston [Ryerson's] Station on Wheeling Creek and he then belonged to the army some time afterwards.[101]

Bain said that he lived on Tenmile Creek in 1781 and that his father's house was burned by Indians destroying the records of his birth. At some point he moved to Virginia near the Ohio, then after the Indian war, he moved to Ohio, settling first along the Captina in Belmont County:

> There were only three families living in that neighborhood at that time [1798], viz., Daniel Bean, who used to roam the forests clothed after the Indian fashion, his brother, — Bean, and Robert Latty.[102]

He then moved a little farther west to near Calais in present-day Monroe County; in 1820 he was listed as a resident of Bloom Township in Morgan County. He was one of the first supervisors of the town of Gaysport, Muskingum County, and was in court over a suit with the Lawrence Allwine, one of the first justices of the peace. With the exception of Vincent (born 1797, probably in Virginia), all of Daniel's children—John, Delilia, Keziah, Sarah, Daniel, Jr., Bryson, Elizabeth and Andrew—were born in Ohio by his first wife. At age sixty-eight, Daniel married his second wife, Susannah Elson. In 1833 he submitted his pension application from Muskingum County and was awarded $60 per annum for his Revolutionary War service from 1781 to 1783.[103] His papers were submitted under the name "Daniel Bean" and Daniel signed with his mark. Since neither Daniel nor his brother John could write, their names appear in the records under various phonetic spellings: Bane, Bean, Been and Bain. John's son, Elisha, who was literate, wrote his name "Bain," and most of Daniel's and John's descendants adopted that spelling of the name.

Like many of the early frontiersmen, Daniel apparently had difficulty adjusting to "civilized" Ohio. He and Abe Hughes as well as others clung to "the dress of the old hunters" and eventually migrated farther west:

> In addition to the Hugheses, may be remembered as old hunters and early frontiersmen, and spies and trailsmen, Dan Bean, Dave Fouts, Old Man Choate, and others, who lingered behind to watch with no great degree of approval the rapid advances of civilization and improvement made by the intruders who had squatted down among them.... The old hunters lingered among us as long as they could well bear with the intruders. Finally, they took up their rifles and traps, being about the amount of their worldly goods, and departed on the trail of his red man, towards the setting sun, to find a more plentiful and unmolested range for the pursuit of their favorite operations.[104]

Daniel "lingered" until 1837, when he sold his land in Muskingum County and headed west. He filed for a change of residence for his pension to Marion County, Indiana, in 1837; to Sangamon County, Illinois, in 1839; and to Des Moines County, Iowa, in 1840. Daniel died in Burlington, Iowa, on November 1, 1840. His widow filed for his benefits in 1853, and then in 1857 she applied for bounty land and was awarded 160 acres.[105]

JOHN BAIN (c1770-1848) was born in Virginia before the Bain family settled in Washington County, Pennsylvania, in the early 1770s. John, or "Jack" as he was often called, was a brother of Daniel and Jesse Bain and the brother-in-law of Charles Craycraft.[106] Their father may have been John Bain, Sr.—the "John Bain" who signed a petition to the Continental Congress (about 1780) to create a new state ("Westsylvania") from the area west of the Alleghenies; the "John Been" in Strabane Township in 1781 taxed for two horses, two cows and five sheep (but no land); and the "John Bean" who served in Lieutenant Brice Virgin's Washington County militia company in 1782. He was probably along on General Brodhead's Coshocton expedition in 1781, as indicated by a receipt to "John Been for Indian corn." This elder John was taxed for personal property in Strabane Township nearly every year from 1781 to 1789. In the 1790 Washington County census he is listed in with a household of three males and four females.

Five Bane brothers—Ellis, Jesse, Nathan, Isaac and Joseph, Jr.—came over to Washington County from the Cacapon River in Hampshire County, Virginia. They settled close to each other on the Bane fork of Tenmile Creek, south of Washington in Amwell Township.[107] These Banes were among the early members of North Ten Mile Baptist Church, along with Enochs. At this time, however, none of the five Bane brothers can be connected to the family of John and Daniel Bain, although the fact that both families were living within a few miles of each other and came to Washington County from the Hampshire-Frederick County area of Virginia suggests that they were related in some manner.

Additional information about John Bain is provided in a letter written by his son, Elisha Bain:

> Having received a letter from you asking me to send you some information attached to the History of my Fathers Life, he was Born in Virginia, the County I Forget, in the Year AD 1774 and Thomahawked by the Indians at the age of Eight Years and Entered the Service of the United States at about seventeen and served under Captin Enix in Defending the Frontier. Then under Captiny Morgan, the Year I do not know. He was wounded in the Service, I think under Enix. Finally, he Settled and Died in the Same Township as whare I now reside [Brookfield Township, Noble County, Ohio] in 1848. My Uncrel Daniel [Bain] Removed to Iowa and Died. I cannot give you their Address for I do not know whare they live. I forgot to say that at the Same time my Father was Thomahawked, he had two Sisters Killed. One was Dead when they found her and the other Died a few Days after.

This is the whole I remember of John Bain, commonly called Jack.[108]

John served in the Rangers following the Revolutionary War and achieved some reputation as a "spy." He was with Enoch's company at Captina Creek in May 1791 and then with Captain Joseph Brock's company at Baker's Fort in June or July of 1791, when he was wounded in both thighs. John was sufficiently recovered in 1792 to return to the militia; Arthur Scott was the captain of the Ranger company; John's brother-in-law, Charles Craycraft, was lieutenant.[109]

On April 10, 1800, John Bain married Hannah Collins in Jefferson County, Ohio (which then included part of Belmont County). He is found with his brother Daniel in Morgan County in 1820 and Muskingum County in 1830. John's homeplace was just south of Cumberland (in present-day Noble County).[110] John Bain died November 28, 1848, and was buried in the "Baptist Cemetery" one mile from Cumberland. The 1850 census for Morgan County lists Hannah Bain, age 70, with a household that included Sarah, 35; Jane, 33; Dorcus, 31; Ann, 29; Zachariah, 27; Lorinda, 12; and Alva, 8. Elisha Bain was a known son (from the above letter), and there may have been others.[111]

(There was another John Bane who settled in Ohio County, Virginia, at the mouth of Short Creek, north of Wheeling, in about 1776. He may be the John Bane listed as a tithable in Ohio County in 1788.[112])

JOSEPH BIGGS (1762-1833) was one of six brothers— William, Benjamin, Jr., Joseph, John, Thomas and Zaccheus— who settled near West Liberty in Ohio County and were all well-known Indian fighters on the frontier. Two of Joseph's brothers were killed by Indians; John was captured and burned during Crawford's disastrous Sandusky expedition in 1782 and Thomas was killed on the Tuscarawas River in Ohio while on a scout. Brother Benjamin was an officer in the Revolutionary War and served throughout the Indian Wars; he was usually referred to as

General Biggs. The Biggs family came west with Benjamin, Sr. (1723-1785), in about 1769 from the Monocacy River in Frederick County, Maryland. A number of their Maryland neighbors migrated to the same area, including members of the Wetzel, Bonnet, Sykes, Hedges and Ogle families.

Joseph was reported to have been at Baker's Fort and treated John Bain's wounds after swimming across the Ohio below Captina. This was the incident at Baker's Fort in June or July 1791. At about the same time as the Captina affair, Joseph would be badly wounded by the Indians in an attack on the Ohio County Rangers at Kirkwood's cabin, near Wheeling. In October of 1791 Biggs was still under the care of Dr. Absalom Baird in Washington County and was boarding with George McColloch. Biggs received an invalid pension in Brooke County, Virginia; he was on the list of Revolutionary War pensioners taken in 1813, drawing $108 per year for service as an ensign.

Biggs lived for a time at the mouth of Grave Creek—he purchased a lot in Elizabethtown (Moundsville) on December 2, 1799—and later moved to Ohio. He requested his pension be transferred to Belmont County in 1825. Jeremiah Hollister recalled him living there:

> [A]s to Joseph Biggs I know him well. He resided about one mile up Pipe Creek and owned a water grist mill. My father moved to the mouth of Captina in April 1809. I was thirteen years old and frequently went to Biggs's Mill. Biggs would take his dram and was a great talker. He was a Lietenant and was wounded in the arm. His arm was badly broken and he drew an invalid pension.[113]

A story was told in West Liberty of Biggs's last visit in 1832.

> Captain Joe Biggs ... returned to West Liberty temporarily on a visit to his relatives and friends, and stopped at the house of Allen Biggs, who at the time kept an inn in the village, but who on the occasion of his visit was absent from home on business. He had left in charge ... a

young man who Mrs. Biggs took aside and instructed to give to the visitant the best liquor there was in the bar.... After indulging in two or three drinks the captain walked on to the porch in front of the house, and shrugging his shoulders (a habit common to him and in which he unconsciously indulged on all occasions) turning to the young man who had accompanied him to the porch, he pointed in the direction of Wheeling and remarked, "I have been in seventeen fights and engagements with Indians at different times between here and Wheeling."[114]

Biggs did not elaborate on the incidents, but asked after his relatives, reminisced for a while about old times, then went on his way. He died the next year in Monroe County, Ohio. His widow, Mary (sister of John Dailey), applied for his pension but was turned down on a technicality; she had not married Joseph before 1794 as required by the pension law.[115]

ALEXANDER BOGGS (1766-1820) was the son of an Irish immigrant, Ezekiel Boggs. Ezekiel came to America as a boy. His family settled first in Newcastle County, Delaware, then moved to Chester County, Pennsylvania. Ezekiel married Jane Johnson and moved to the "western country," settling on Buffalo Creek. He appears on the tax list for Donegal Township, Washington County, in 1781 and is listed as a tithable in Ohio County, Virginia, in 1786 and 1788. Ezekiel died in Belmont County, Ohio, in 1815.

Ezekiel's son Alexander married Hannah Martin in 1792. Alexander and his brother William were among the earliest settlers on Indian Wheeling Creek in Belmont County. William lived near Newelstown (now St. Clairsville) and was a supervisor of Kirkwood Township; in 1833 he migrated to Knox County and died there in 1848. Alexander was elected to serve as a county commissioner from 1806 to 1807, and from 1811 to 1820. The

1813 fall election was marred by an incident that ended well for Boggs:

> Alexander Boggs and Sterling Johnson were the rival candidates before the sovereigns of Belmont County for the responsible office of commissioner. The canvassers, for a supposed defeat, threw out the poll box of Pultney Township [where Boggs lived], thereby securing the election of Johnson. He did not long enjoy the dignitaries of office, for Boggs, nothing daunted, proceeded to contest the election. On the 18th day of said month and year, the court "ousted" Johnson and awarded the station to Boggs, who was much set up at his triumph.[116]

After Boggs's death in Belmont County, his heirs sued each other over division of 254 acres that he had owned. The suit named Alexander's widow Hannah and the following children: Ezekiel of Richland County and James, Reuben, Margaret, Jane, Elizabeth, Francis, Alice, Lucinda, William and Alexander, all of Belmont County.[117]

JOHN DAILEY (c1770-1843) stated in a deposition that in 1782 he lived on Tenmile Creek near Jackson's Fort (later Waynesville in Greene County) and that two or three years later his family moved to Wheeling. He also stated that he was serving under Captain Brock at the time of the Indian attack on Baker's Fort (June or July 1791). Dailey may have gone back and forth between Ohio County and Washington County in his early years. A "John Dailey" appears on the militia pay rolls of both counties. In 1794 Dailey served eight months in Captain James Seals's company in Washington County; he signed his pay roll voucher—$48.58 for time served and "for the use of my gun"—with his mark.

Sometime after the treaty was signed ending the Indian war, Dailey located near the mouth of Captina Creek in Ohio. He or his father, James Dailey, may have claimed the property where John was tending corn in 1791; however, records show neither owning land in that area. In 1802 John moved from Captina and settled permanently near what is now Calias in Monroe County. He was one of the first settlers of Seneca Township, which was organized in 1815, and he is credited with laying out the first town there—Calais—in 1837. John Dailey and his wife, Nancy, are listed in the 1830 census for Monroe County with a household of ten.[118]

ABRAHAM ENOCH (-1791) commanded the Rangers at the battle of Captina, but aside from his role in this affair, little is known about him. He was a son of Henry Enoch, Sr., an early settler of the Tenmile country (c1769), who lived at the forks of Tenmile Creek near present-day Clarksville in Greene County, Pennsylvania. The family had a long history of military service on the western frontier. Henry, Sr., served as an officer throughout the Revolutionary War and later rose to the rank of lieutenant colonel in the Washington County militia. Militia rolls show that his sons Henry, Jr., and William Enoch served under him, but there is no record of Abraham in the militia during this time (1781-85). It is possible that Abraham was the "Abram Ennix" (also spelled "Abm Ennicks") in James O'Hara's Virginia company at Fort Pitt in 1777.

As recalled by John Shoptaw, in 1791 Abraham was elected ensign of a Washington County militia company, his brother William was elected the lieutenant, and Henry the captain. Abraham's death was long remembered by those who lived on the frontier. Over fifty years after Captina, Mrs. Phebe Miranda of Warren County, Ohio, recalled in an interview with Lyman Draper that "Abraham Enoch was a son of Captain Henry Enoch and while yet a young man was killed by Indians." Phebe, a daughter of Benjamin Stites, had lived near Henry Enoch on Tenmile; she was seventeen years old when the battle occurred.[119]

HENRY ENOCH (1748-1825) was the son of Henry Enoch of Washington County, Pennsylvania, and the grandson of Henry Enoch of Hampshire County, Virginia. The grandfather settled at the forks of the Cacapon River and the father at the forks of Tenmile Creek. Henry III—whom we shall refer to here as Henry, Jr.—obtained from his grandfather a tract of land located on the Monongahela River in Fayette County, and he obtained from his father—Henry, Sr.—at least one tract located on Tenmile Creek. Henry, Jr., was involved in extensive business dealings with his father and brothers, at the forks of Tenmile. After his father died in 1797, the bulk of the estate must have gone to Henry, Jr. According to one historian, in 1798

> Henry paid the highest tax among 160 taxpayers in Morgan Township, Greene County, where he lived in a twenty-four by thirty-foot two-story log house with nine twelve-paned windows valued at $200 which was high for a log house.[120]

By that time, the family businesses were foundering and in 1799 the sheriff put the assets of Henry, William and their brother Isaac up for sale.

Henry married Elizabeth Teagarden from the neighboring family on Tenmile Creek. Sometime after 1800 they left Pennsylvania and went down the Ohio to settle for a time near the mouth of the Little Kanawha, before relocating to Montgomery County, Ohio. His name appears frequently in the court records of Wayne Township from 1808 until 1820. He is listed in the 1820 census for Montgomery County; in 1830 his name is missing and there is an entry for "widow" Enoch.[121]

Extensive military service is documented for Henry, Jr., all in the militia Washington County, Pennsylvania. He appears as a private on the roll for Captain Andrew Fairley's company in 1782 and also on undated rolls in Captain Benjamin Stites company, Lieutenant James Blackburns's company and Ensign David Ruble's company. In January 1792 Governor Mifflin commissioned the officers elected for Washington County, including Henry, Jr., lieutenant of the 1st Company. In February the governor was informed that Lieutenant Enoch had declined his appointment; possibly, he was still affected by his brother's death the previous

May. Henry, however, did return to service and in 1793 was commissioned again, this time as major, commanding officer of the 2nd Battalion of the 2nd Regiment.[122]

WILLIAM ENOCH (1762-1836), another son of Henry Enoch, was born on his grandfather's plantation in Hampshire County, Virginia. William owned a tract called "Hazard" adjoining his father on Tenmile Creek. William and his brother Isaac invested heavily in the "industrialization" of the forks: they built an iron works, grist mill, sawmill and other improvements on land they obtained from their father. Business was booming at first. To hire woodcutters to feed their furnace—one of the earliest west of the Alleghenies—they ran an advertisement in the local newspaper in 1797:

> Wood Cutters and Labourers wanted by William and Isaac Enoch at the "new furnace" on the North Fork of Ten Mile; cash will be given—3 shillings 6 pence per cord to those who will cut 100 cords of wood.[123]

About the same year, William married Mary Tegarden, who had grown up near the Enochs on Tenmile Creek. The budding family empire was in shambles, and at April Court, 1799, "the sheriff of Greene County took over and proceeded to sell the assets available."

After the Enochs' business failures, the couple left Washington County and settled at the mouth of Little Kanawha (present-day Parkersburg), probably a little before his brother Henry arrived. William's occupation there was listed as blacksmith and gunsmith. He appears in the court records of Wood County from 1801 to 1805 and was a member of the militia in 1806-07. The family then removed to Clark County, Ohio, where they were early settlers of German Township (1808). William took an active part in local affairs. He was appointed an associate judge of the county and was even reported as one of "those who are known to have been out in the war" of 1812. He and Mary raised ten children, all but one of which were born in Ohio.

William served in the Washington County Rangers for over a decade. The earliest service found for him is about 1782, when he is listed as a private in Captain Benjamin Stites's company, along with his brother Henry, Jr., and neighbor Levi Harrod. In 1793 he is shown on a return as captain in the 2nd Regiment of Washington County. His brother Henry is listed as major and two brother-in-laws, Benjamin Bell and Joseph Avecost, are listed as captains, all serving in the same regiment. The copy of a commission signed by Governor Mifflin shows William was a major in 1795. Finally, in 1796 William is listed as a major in the 2nd Regiment, and his younger brother Isaac is listed as a captain.[124]

DUNCAN McARTHUR (1772-1840) was the son of a Scottish immigrant, who grew up on the frontier of western Pennsylvania and later became the eleventh governor of Ohio. John McArthur came to New York before 1746, and his son Duncan was born in Duchess County. After his wife died in 1775, John remarried and moved to Washington County, Pennsylvania. In 1785 John McArthur obtained a patent for 399 acres in West Finley Township. His tract, adjoining the lands of Hercules and James Roney, was located near the head of Middle Wheeling Creek, about twelve miles southwest of Washington. The McArthurs were a poor family when they came from New York and did not prosper in Pennsylvania. In 1787 the *Pittsburgh Gazette* carried an announcement that McArthur's farm, which he had secured on a mortgage from the general loan office of Pennsylvania, was to be sold for debt. Duncan, the oldest of a number of children, was hired out to work on their neighbors' farms and in the process received minimal formal schooling. Eighteen-year-old McArthur received his first military experience as a volunteer in Harmar's campaign of 1790. He was elected ensign in Captain Hercules Roney's militia company in 1792. Hercules Roney built an early blockhouse on his farm for protection from the Indians.

Duncan McArthur left Washington County as a young man and moved to Maysville, Kentucky, where he was employed for a time at a salt works. In 1792 he joined Nathaniel Massie surveying in the Scioto River valley of Ohio, which was then in the midst of Indian country. During the peace that followed the treaty of Greenville, he helped Massie lay out the city of Chillicothe (1796) and selected a farm north of the town to settle on. McArthur was described as being "tall in stature with a giant frame and possessed speed on foot which saved his life on several occasions." According to another description:

> Duncan McArthur was a son of nature. His hair was black as a raven, and his eyes dark and piercing. When excited there was an unearthly flash in his fiery eye which indicated a keen and daring spirit, restless and fearless.[125]

McArthur entered politics in 1804, when he was elected as a representative of Ross County. He served in the house from 1804 to 1805, and in the senate from 1805 to 1813. In the War of 1812, he led an Ohio regiment to Detroit and was taken prisoner following General Hull's surrender. McArthur was paroled by the British and, shortly after, elected to Congress. In 1813 he was appointed to the rank of brigadier general and resigned his seat in Congress to re-enter the army. McArthur served under General William Henry Harrison, whom he succeeded in command of the Northwest army. When the war ended McArthur retired briefly to his farm.

Now one of the most noted and popular figures in the Scioto valley, McArthur was soon called back to public service. In 1815 he was returned to the legislature, and in 1816 appointed by the war department as a commissioner to the treaty negotiations with the Northwest Indian nations. In 1817 he was reelected to the legislature and was chosen as the speaker of the house. McArthur was returned to the Congress in 1822 for one term. In 1830 he resigned his seat in the state senate to run for governor of Ohio on the National Republican ticket—winning by less than 500 votes. His administration focused on internal improvements—construction of the barge canals and completion of the National

Road from Wheeling to Zanesville. After one two-year term he retired again to Ross County.

In 1797 McArthur married Nancy McDonald, and they had eleven children. Nancy was the sister of John McDonald, McArthur's biographer. They all made their homes in Ross County, Ohio. The McArthur residence near Chillicothe was known as "Fruit Hill" and was a gathering place of the political figures and celebrities of his day. He achieved considerable wealth from his diverse business activities, which included iron furnaces, mills and real estate. His wife died in 1836, and McArthur died on his farm a few years later.[126]

GEORGE McCOLLOCH   A McColloch family emigrated from the South Branch of the Potomac and settled on Wheeling Creek. There were four brothers, Samuel, John, Abraham and George, as well as a sister, Elizabeth, who married Ebenezer Zane. The brothers performed illustrious service on the frontier during the Revolutionary War. Samuel was famed for his "leap" from the summit of Wheeling Hill during the Indian attack of 1777. Brother George appears on the 1788 tax list for Ohio County. He was a justice of the peace for the county and one of the first trustees of West Liberty, which was established in 1787. George had a son, George, Jr., and both father and son are named in John Newbury's will of 1777, the first will probated in Ohio County. "George McCulloch" (probably the son) is listed on a pay roll of the Ohio County militia in 1791. In October 1791, "George McColloch" signed a receipt for expenses he incurred "boarding and nursing" Elijah Hedges (wounded at Kirkwood's cabin) for the previous twenty-three weeks at $3 per week. George McCulloch, Jr., was one of the scouts for Ohio County in 1792 and 1793; a muster roll of the "spies" for 1792 lists him as age twenty-two, single, residing at "Wheelin," and indicates that he was appointed on August 12 to serve in place of Martin Wetzel, who mustered out on August 2. According to Samuel Hedges, the younger George McColloch "killed an Indian in the War of 1812, between Mansfield and Greentown," and then

George "died on the way to Lower Sandusky to join Harrison during the War of 1812." Hedges related a number of anecdotes about this George McColloch and stated that he was the one involved in the battle of Captina.[127]

Making matters interesting, there was another family of this name in Washington County. This family, usually spelled "McCullough," emigrated from Lancaster County, Pennsylvania, to Smith Township, Washington County, where George McCullough was the foreman of a grand jury in 1775 and patented a tract called "Gretna Green" in 1785. Two George McCulloughs are listed in the 1790 Washington County census. One of these lived in Smith Township and died there in 1811. In 1782, two men named "George McCulloch," a Senior and a Junior, served in the Washington County militia in Captain Andrew Swearingham's company. A "George McCullough" was killed "by the Indians on the lower side of the great Miami [in Ohio]" in 1793; this information comes from an interview with Samuel McDowell, who also described several adventures of Duncan McArthur.[128]

Evidence favors George McColloch as the Ranger at Captina, and the case is strengthened by a statement to this effect by Samuel Hedges who knew George personally.

ADAM MILLER (c1766-1791) Other than his participation at Captina and burial at Baker's Fort, little has been learned of Adam Miller. Quite a bit is known about Adam's family. He was the son of Jacob Miller, Sr., of Donegal Township, Washington County. Jacob was probably the "Jacob Muller" who arrived at Philadelphia in 1753 with his brother Christopher. Jacob may have settled briefly in Maryland before locating at the Dutch Fork Settlement of Donegal Township in about 1775. On Easter Sunday, March 31, 1782, Jacob Miller and John Hupp, while out looking for a lost colt near Miller's blockhouse, were killed by a party of about twenty Shawnee warriors. The two men were buried in the Miller cemetery, just east of Dutch Fork Lake, where Jacob's wife and some of his children were later interred.

Washington County Orphan Court records give the name of Jacob's wife (Mary) and children (Mary, Jacob, John, Adam, Catherine, Frederick, Peter and Henry). Adam's older brother, Jacob, Jr., was elected captain of a Washington County militia company in 1793.[129]

Adam Miller is listed in the 1790 census for Washington County as the head of a household with one female. The history for Jacob Miller's family indicates that Adam never married. Adam was taxed in Washington County from 1788 to 1791. He received a share of his father's estate on August 1, 1786, and was present when the land was divided in 1788. The three eldest brothers—Jacob, John and Adam—each received 266 acres. Adam had scouting experience prior to Captina; he was paid for his services as a spy by the Supreme Executive Council of Pennsylvania on December 10, 1789. He was a scout again in the spring of 1791, being appointed by the county lieutenant, James Marshel. Following Adam's death, his land was transferred on his younger brother, Frederick.[130]

JOHN SHOPTAW (1764-before 1850) The Shoptaw family (later spelled Shoptaugh) migrated from Virginia to Kentucky, stopping in western Pennsylvania along the way. John Shoptaw, Sr., was one of the inhabitants of Somerset Township, Washington County, in 1781; he is on the tax roll for 80 acres, two horses, two cows and six sheep. After residing there for a few years, the family moved at various times to Nelson County, Kentucky. The dates can be determined from the Nelson County tax lists: there are no Shoptaws in 1787; a John and William in 1790; and a William, John and John Sr. in 1792. The "John Shaptaw" listed in the 1790 Washington County, Pennsylvania, census is no doubt John, Jr., the one involved in the battle of Captina.

Personal information about John Shoptaw, Jr., is found in his pension application, submitted from Bullitt County, Kentucky, where he lived in 1832. He was born March 11, 1764, in Berkeley County, Virginia, and moved to Washington County, Pennsylvania, with his father. John, Jr., first enlisted in the militia there under Captain Jenkins and Lieutenant Peter Drake in 1788. During his tour of one month and one week, he rendezvoused at Lindley's Mills and served as a spy on the frontiers. In 1791 he volunteered again, serving a six-month tour in the militia. After enlisting in March, Colonel James Marshel appointed Shoptaw one of the spies for Washington County. Of the three spies commissioned with him, two were killed by the Indians at Captina (Adam Miller and Isaac McCowan) and one was captured (John Daniels). Shoptaw received a discharge from Marshel in September. John Shoptaw's application for a Revolutionary War pension was rejected due to the fact that his service was in the "Indian War" and not the Revolution.

In the fall of 1791 John, Jr., left Pennsylvania and joined the rest of his family in Nelson County, Kentucky. There he lived near his sister Catherine and brothers William, Andrew and Henry. He owned 50 acres on Froman Creek and 77 acres on West Cox Creek; this area is near the present Nelson-Bullitt county line, northwest of Bardstown. He also owned 250 acres on Little Beech Creek in Shelby County, about twenty-five miles northeast of his land on Froman and West Cox creeks. John had at least one son, John Shoptaw III.[131]

JOHN YOHO (1775-1853) was a grandson of the immigrant, Johannes Yoho, who came to America in 1738 from the Alsace region between France and Switzerland. Two of Johannes' sons—Henry and Peter—settled in western Pennsylvania in the early 1770s, where they were closely associated with the Baker family. Henry and Peter Yoho married Catherine and Margaret Baker, twin daughters of Captain John Baker. The two brothers settled on Fish Creek by 1788 and both died in present-day Marshall County, West Virginia. John Yoho, a son of Peter, may have been living near Baker's Fort in 1791, as he stated that he was working on a blockhouse there in June or July when the fort was attacked. John married Mary Cits (or Kitts) in Jefferson County, Ohio, in 1801 and later settled in Sunbury Township,

An Inquiry into the Captina Affair

Monroe County. He was listed there in the 1820 census with wife Mary and nine children and died there, leaving a will, in 1853.[132]

A number of the participants at Captina cannot be positively identified. More research is needed to learn where these men came from and what happened to those who survived. Some data are provided below which may help to locate them. The author would appreciate hearing from anyone with additional information or sources.

JOHN DANIELS In 1862 Lyman Draper wrote to Jeremiah Hollister, inquiring "What became of John Daniels after his return from captivity?" Hollister replied, "As to John Daniels I have no knowledge but will refer you to Isaac Baker," whom Hollister said was living in Taswell County, Illinois. Draper's extensive papers may hold some other reference to Daniels, but I have been unable to find any.

A John Daniels of Washington County is on the pay abstract of Levi Harrod's Ranger company in 1782 (along with Henry Enoch, Jr.) and the pay roll for Captain James Seals' Ranger company in 1794 (Charles Craycraft, ensign; John Dailey, Henry Enoch and Enoch Enoch, Jr., privates; the latter two being sons of Enoch Enoch). In May 1795 "John Danills" signed (by his mark) a pay receipt for service in Captain Seals' company. A John Daniels is also found on the 1785 tax list for Morgan Township, Washington County.

"John Daniels" is not found in the 1790 Washington County census; however, there is a "John Donald" with a household of one male and seven females, as well as a "Henry Donald." Crumrine writes of a John Donnell and his father, Henry, who came to Washington County in 1776 from Winchester, Virginia. John received a Virginia certificate for 400 acres, located in Cecil Township, where he resided. The certificate was made out for "John Daniel." This John Donnell married Rebecca Evans of Amwell Township.[133]

DOBBINS Three Dobbinses are listed in the 1790 Washington County census: James, John and Lennard. James Dobbins patented 400 acres in Smith Township; in 1798 he was a lieutenant in the First Brigade of the Washington County militia; and he is listed in the 1800 Washington County census (age 26-45) with a wife and one daughter.

There were two "Dobbinses" that received pensions for Revolutionary War service in Pennsylvania: James Dobbins was awarded a pension, and John Dobbins's widow received a pension. James Dobbins (born about 1757) lived near Canonsburg in Washington County after the Revolutionary War and later moved to Westmoreland County. John Dobbins (born about 1747) married Elizabeth Keener on Whitely Creek (in present-day Greene County) and later moved to Hampshire County, Virginia.[134]

DOWNING In 1781 the Downings—John, James and Timothy—were all residents of Hopewell Township, but all of the family eventually left Washington County. Timothy Downing was a well-known frontier scout, who moved to Kentucky in about 1790. He was a captain of the Rangers in Washington County in 1782; a muster roll for his company lists privates Robert and James Downing. In 1792 or 1793, Captain James Downing was recommended for appointment as one of the "spies" of Ohio County, Virginia, in a petition by "the inhabitants of the upper part of the said County." Howe described an incident that occurred in the area of present-day Stark County, Ohio, involving James Downing, Sr. In April 1793 Downing—described as being "past middle age and somewhat fleshy"—was out on a scout with four other Rangers. One morning before breakfast they were jumped by eighteen to twenty Ottawa and Wyandot. The Indians struck from two sides, but the Rangers all made their escape. Howe said all five men, Downing included, later moved to Stark County.

All of the Downings apparently had left the area by the late 1880s; none are listed in the 1790 Washington County census or the 1788 Ohio County tax list. Several Downeys were awarded pensions or bounty lands for Revolutionary War service in Pennsylvania—John, Patrick, Samuel and Thomas.[135]

HOFFMAN (-1791) No first name was given for the "Hoffman" killed at Captina. Numerous Huffmans are listed in the 1790 census for Washington County: Christian, David, George, Henry, John and Rudolph. Rudolph Huffman was a prominent resident of Somerset Township, where he was the proprietor of a well-known distillery. The distillery and mill are still standing (1994) near Cokeburg. The Huffmans were probably German, which may account for one of the Captina accounts referring to the slain Hoffman as a "Dutchman." Henry and John Huffman are found on the militia rolls for Washington County for 1781-82. Several Huffman/Hoffman women in Pennsylvania were awarded Revolutionary War pensions or bounty lands on behalf of their deceased husbands, but none of these fit a veteran who died in 1791.

A biography for Rossbury Huffman of Monroe County, Ohio, where many Washington County families moved after 1800, states that "his uncle, Phillip Huffman, was supposed to have been killed by the Indians; he was in the army and never returned." a tantalizing clue, it may refer to Philip of the Virginia Line who was killed in the Revolutionary War and whose heirs were awarded bounty land warrants. [136]

JOHN LINE (-1791) The brothers John Line and Joseph Line of Washington County, Pennsylvania, were veterans of the Revolutionary War. The family (name also spelled Lines) appears in the early tax lists for Morgan Township, which also lists a Samuel Line. A militia roll for Captain Andrew Fairley's company, recruited on Castille Run (in present-day Greene County) lists Joseph Line as sergeant and John, Samuel and William as privates. Considerable personal information is available for John and Joseph in their pension applications. Joseph was born in New Jersey in 1755, and John in about 1757. In 1777 both men enlisted on Tenmile Creek for service under Captain William Harrod in George Rogers Clark's western campaign. They were marched to Wheeling, rafted to Louisville where they built a fort, and then on to the Illinois country where they participated in the taking of Kaskaskia and Vincennes. They also participated in Colonel William Crawford's defeat. John married Mary Baltzell and Joseph married Mary Magdalena Hoost; they later removed with their families to Shelby County, Ohio, and were awarded pensions for their war service. John died in 1834, Joseph in 1837; both men and their wives are buried in Medaris Cemetery in Perry Township.[137]

John, Joseph, William and Samuel Line could have had adult children living in Washington County in 1791. The pension files and D.A.R. records list a number of the "surviving children" of John and Joseph, but do not mention a son John. The John Line killed at Captina could have belonged to one of these families.

ISAAC and ABRAHAM McCOWAN (-1791) In the Captina accounts, the surname is spelled McCoun, McCowan, McKeown and McKeon. No persons of these names are found on militia rolls, tax lists or the 1790 Washington County census. William Harrod, Jr., gave the names of both Isaac and Abraham, so he may have been acquainted with these men in his neighborhood or he may have served with them in the militia. The 1781 tax rolls for Washington County list a John McKowen for Bethlehem Township, Samuel McKown for Cecil Township, Joseph and John McCowan in Hopewell Township, and Joseph McCoun in Nottingham Township. Two McKowns—Samuel and William—were residing in Washington County in 1800.[138]

JOHN SUTHERLAND There was a John Sutherland in the 1790 Washington County, Pennsylvania, census. This is probably John Sutherland, Sr., of West Finley Township, a native of Scotland and widower, who came to America in about 1773 with his son George and daughter Barbara. To pay his passage, he bound himself to a planter near Bladensburg, Maryland. He married Margaret Morrow and came to Washington County in about 1783. John and Margaret had sons George, John, Jr., Daniel, Alexander and David. In 1834, while residing in Cross Creek Township, John Sutherland applied for a Revolutionary War pension. He stated that he was born in about 1748, enlisted in the Maryland line in 1775, and was at the battle of Brandywine and at the storming of Stony Point. John died in 1842 and is buried in Cross Creek Cemetery (tombstone has 1751-1842).

In 1794 John Sutherland, Jr., took an oath of allegience to the United States in Fallowfield Township, Washington County. Jeremiah Hollister provides a clue which suggests that John, Jr., may have been the one involved at Captina. In a letter to Draper, Hollister wrote that

> I know nothing of those men you mention except John Sutherland. I was personally acquainted with his brother David Sutherland, but John I believe lived and died on Fish Creek Virginia.[139]

John, Jr., did have a brother David, but no John Sutherland appears in census records in the area drained by Fish Creek. There was a John Sutherland who settled a little further down river, in Wood County, Virginia, and first appears there in the 1810 census.[140]

TATE   There are no Tates in early Washington County. A John Tate is listed as a tithable in Ohio County, Virginia, in 1788. Sometime in July of 1792, a tragedy occurred a little upstream known as the Tate family massacre. The family lived about 250 yards below Dille's Fort and across the river from the Grave Creek settlement. The incident began when "old Mr. Tate" was shot by Indians as he stepped out the door of his cabin. The Indians rushed the cabin and once inside killed several children and Tate's daughter-in-law.[141]

RAY VENNAM   Nicholas Van Eman, a native of Holland, came to Washington County with his family and settled on Little

Chartiers Creek in Somerset Township. Nicholas died in 1781, leaving four sons—George, Nicholas, Andrew and Garrett. There are four Vinneman households listed in the 1790 Washington County census: George, Andrew, Solomon and "widow Vinneman." George Vineman sat on the first grand jury of Washington County. This family is also found on the Washington County militia rolls: Andrew and George Venemon in March-April 1782; George Vanemman and Andrew Venemon in July 1782; George Venems and Garet Vanaman in September 1782; and George Vennoms (no date). The varied spellings are consistent with these names all belonging to the same family. Andrew, George and Nicholas Venneman lived "on the waters of Chartiers Creek," where they had adjoining tracts in Somerset and Strabane townships. Garrett removed to Kentucky by 1781.

Andrew Vaneman married Elizabeth Riddle in 1788; he was awarded a pension for Revolutionary War service in Pennsylvania and died in Washington County. Andrew stated in his pension application that he was born in Wilmington, Delaware, in 1750, moved with his family first to near Hagerstown, Maryland, and then to Washington County, Pennsylvania, in about 1776. He was a volunteer in Crawford's expedition of 1782. Andrew served at various other times on the frontier, although he could not recollect the dates; he said he served at Holliday's Cove under Captain Matthew Ritchie, at Van Meter's Fort on Short Creek and at Mingo Bottom under Lieutenant Hugh Forbes, and also "opposite the mouth of Big Beaver" and at a station at the head of Wheeling Creek [possibly Ryerson's Station]. He continued to reside in Somerset Township, Washington County, following the war and received his pension there. Andrew saw regular service on the frontier after the war in a unit commanded by Daniel Hamilton:

> There were frequent calls for men . . . during all the period from 1783 to 1790 . . . and in most or perhaps all of those calls, he well recollects of seeing the said Andrew Vanemon provided and equiped for service and that he

did perform the several tours of duty in the years above mentioned and for each of which they were allowed as for one month service.[142]

One of the Vaneman/Van Eman family could have been the "Vennam" at Captina. A "Ray" has not been identified in this family, and Ray was an extremely uncommon name at that time. Andrew would be one likely candidate, as he stated that "from the commencement of the Indian war till its termination, I was frequently out in the service of the United States, either as a volunteer or as a drafted militia man against the Indians on the frontier."[143]

The description of the Captina affair in the present work is entirely from the point of view of the whites, because theirs are the only available accounts. In the absence of written Native American records we can only imagine how the events at Captina were perceived by the Shawnee. None of the Indians who were involved are known, with one exception—Charley Wilkey. Fortunately, we do have some biographical data for him, which was provided by John McDonald.

CHARLEY WILKEY Wilkey was the only Native American named in the Captina accounts. In his biography of Duncan McArthur, John McDonald indicated that after the peace he became acquainted with a Shawnee chief "known to the whites about Chillicothe by the name of Charley Wilkey." Elsewhere, in an article written for the *Western Christian Advocate*, McDonald gave a brief description of Wilkey, who was described as being a "short, thick, strong, active man with a very agreeable and intelligent countenance." In the fall of 1792, Indians captured the frontier scout Samuel Davis[144] on the Big Sandy River in Kentucky. McDonald said that "this body of Indians was commanded by a Shawnee chief, who called himself Captain Charles Wilky." Davis managed to escape from his captors and afterwards harbored no animosity to Wilkey: "Davis always spoke of him as being kind and humane to him." The Indians and whites in the vicinity of Ross County apparently thought highly of Wilkey also:

> He was communicative and sociable in his manners. The first three or four years after Chillicothe was settled, this Indian mixed freely with the whites and upon no occasion did he show a disposition to be troublesome. He was admitted by the other Indians, who spoke of him, to be a warrior of the first order—fertile in expedients and bold to carry his plans into execution.

On one occasion long after the peace, a number of Indians appeared at Samuel Davis's shop. The party came up to the shop door, and one Indian held out his hand and said, "How do my brother?" Davis took a closer look and recognized "Captain Wilky, the chief who had captured him." McDonald continued with Davis's story:

> As this Indian had uniformly treated him with humanity while he was a prisoner, there was no personal ill will between them. After Captain Wilky shook hands with him, the other Indians in succession received his hand. They had a hearty laugh about Davis knocking down the Indian.

The latter was a reference to Davis's captivity, when he had pushed one of his guards into a campfire and made a daring escape from the Indians.[145]

PART THREE

DOCUMENTARY RECORDS

Accounts of the Captina Affair

The following are transcripts of all the accounts that refer to the Captina affair collected to date by the author. They are presented below in their entirety and are arranged in chronological order.

David Shepherd

David Shepherd (c1734-1795) was born in Frederick County, Virginia, and in 1770 settled at the forks of Big and Little Wheeling, where he built a blockhouse. He was appointed county lieutenant for Ohio County, Virginia, in 1776. During the siege of Fort Henry (Wheeling) in 1777, his son and son-in-law were killed and his fort was burned. Shepherd commanded the Ohio County militia throughout the Revolutionary War and served in the Virginia legislature from 1783 to 1785. Many of Shepherd's numerous papers survived and were obtained by Lyman C. Draper; these papers are now accessible on five rolls of microfilm. The dispatch below is a letter that Shepherd sent to Secretary of War Henry Knox.[146]

Draper MSS 3SS37.[147]

Ohio County, May the 6th 1791

Sir—Agreable to the orders to me Directed I have ordered out the militia agreable to the Enclosed Return, but Since that we find that the Number is not Equal to the present Immergancy. Within a few Days past the Indians have made a general attact on us and have killed Seven of our Scouts, Ensign Enox among the killed and Ensign Biggs among the wounded with Several of the privates. They have made attempts to take two of the Blockhouses but have failed and have killed Several of the Inhabitants the Number not known. We have allarms Every Day. The Barer Captain Kirkwood will be more able to give you a perfect account as he was in one of the princable actions to which I refer you. We are without amunition and but a few arms. Every Day Shews New Seens of Cruelty and the appearance of a general invasion.

I am with due respect, &c.

York General-Advertiser

This article, which appeared in the York General-Advertiser *on May 25, 1791, is the only contemporary account uncovered to date. This newspaper published in York County, Pennsylvania, describes both actions referred to in Colonel David Shepherd's dispatch of May 9—Kirkwood's cabin and Captina Creek. The article also mentions the Crow incident, though not by name, and by placing it last, implies that the Crows were killed after the battle at Captina. The article also implies that the surviving sister, who was Tena Crow, saw the Rangers' scalps carried by one of the Indians. While she may well have seen scalps, it is doubtful that she identified them as Rangers'. It is unlikely that the Crows were killed after Captina.*

Other than the date and location, this Captina account is fairly lacking in detail and presents some problems of "interpretation;" for example, trying to trace all of the modifiers in the second sentence of the second paragraph. The sentence may be taken to mean that one of the Enochs was at Fish Creek Station (Baker's Fort) with a party of Rangers awaiting "information" from his brother, who was on Dunkard Creek (Ryerson's Station) with another party of Rangers. As the article does not indicate that there were two separate incidents, the May 1 date could either be the day the scouts were fired upon or the day Abraham Enoch's company was ambushed on Captina.

One would expect the Captina incident to have been reported in the "local" newspaper for southwest Pennsylvania, the Pittsburgh Gazette. *Unfortunately, copies of the* Gazette *for this period are missing.[148]*

Documentary Records

Diana Bowman, *Pennsylvania Herald and York General Advertiser, Book 1, 1789-1793* (Apollo, Pennsylvania, 1993), pp. 99-100.

Pittsburgh: On April 30th a party of Virginia Rangers, under the direction of Joseph Bigs, who were engaged in building a block house opposite the mouth of Wheeling. They had taken shelter in a cabin near by, where all fell asleep from the fatigue, Indians had set fire to the cabin roof. The Indians stood by the door expecting the people to run out, fortunately Captain Kirkwood succeeded in getting the side of the roof with the fire thrown off, preventing the rest of the house from taking on the fire. The Indians fired between the logs and wounded Mr. Bigs and five others. Mr. Walker one of the wounded has since died. At day break the Indians disappeared, not knowing whether any damage was caused to the Rangers inside.

Washington County: On May 1st a party of Washington County Rangers stationed at the mouth of Fish Creek, discovered some Indians remote from the Ohio. The party of rangers were waiting for information from Lieutenant Enix, who commanded the party on Dunkard Creek, being at the Fish Creek Station, where his brother commanded, called out fifteen volunteers and crossed the river. They soon came in sight of four Indians who fled, until they had completely drawn Mr. Enix into an ambuscade of forty or more, who then fired on them. Mr. Enix ordered his men to take shelter, he and his brave men lost their lives on the spot, with one missing. A party that crossed the river buried Lieutenant Enix and his men, confirmed eight Indians killed.

On that same day three Indians were about three miles from Mr. Ryerson's farm on the Dunkard Creek, took four young girls. They were taken some distance from their home, two were killed and scalped, the third was tomahawked and scalped (died a few days since) and the fourth was knocked down and afterwards made her escape. She affirms that one of the Indians had seven scalps hanging on his pouch.

John Dailey

John Dailey mentioned Captina in two declarations he made in 1832 in support of pension applications. In the first deposition, he describes the occasion when John Bain was wounded at Baker's Fort. This is a separate incident that occurred about two months after the battle of Captina—in late June or early July 1791. Dailey stated that at the time of the Baker's Fort incident he and John Bain both were serving under Captain Brock.

Draper MSS 6ZZ99.

State of Ohio
Monroe County

Personally appeared before me John Linn one of the advocate judges of the Court of Common Please of Monroe County John Dailey who being Duly sworn according to law Deposeth and saith that in the last of June or first of July and he thinks in the year of one thousand seven hundred and ninety one that to his certain knowledge that John Bane and Myself was in the service of Captain Brock and the said Bane was wounded in both thighs, in the left thigh badly and right slightly and by particular circumstances positive that it was Indians. The circumstances was I (John Dailey) was at work tending Corn at the mouth of Captina Creek near Baker's Station on the Ohio River, on the Ohio side, and hired Joseph Baker to assist me in hoeing corn. We went over the River in a Canoe early in the morning, and the said Bane came over to explore round to see if any danger could be apprehended and about ten or eleven Oclock he came to where we was at work and said he wished to go over to the Station. We told him

to go and take our Canoe and he said he would, and started away and in a few Minutes we heard three guns go off, and then almost instantly two, or three more. We made preparations to cross the River over to the Station, and just as we commenced crossing over a man by the name of Honseley Baker hollowed and said "Hurry over. The Indians have killed or shot at John Bane." And we hurried over as fast as possible, and went to the Station about half mile Distance, and there was the said John Bane wounded in both thighs, and the next day we raised some men and went to the place they fired on him, and followed them some distance, and were positive it was Indians, and that the said Bane was in the service of the said Brock, until discharge and further this deponent saith not. Sworn and subscribed before me this nineteenth day of June A.D. 1832.
John Linn, Associate Judge

John Dailey

In the second deposition Dailey gives some personal information and confirms Daniel Bain's presence at the battle of Captina and at the later incident at Baker's Fort. Dailey, who was illiterate, signed the document with his mark; the justice of the peace, Michel Atkinson, wrote the deposition in a crude but readable hand.

Daniel Bean, Revolutionary War pension application, Pennsylvania, W. 8124.

The State of Ohio
Monroe County

John Daley... after being Duly sworne according to Law Deposeth and saith that he Lived and resided at a place called Tin Mile in Pennsylvania. I think it is now in green County. The Summer that Colnoel Crawford was killed by the Indians and his armie Defeted which was in the year 1782 there was at that time one fort arutie [Guthrie?] on whitely and an other fort called Jack-

sons fort on Ten mile and Some distance north from that, say about eight or nine miles, was an other fort called Atkinson fort[149] and I have understood by an number since that Major Charles Craycraft[150] commanded at Atkinsons fort. About two or three years after wards my father and family moved down to Wheelin in Virginia. I was about fifteen years old at that time. I there became acquainted with Daniel Bean. He was Living there at the fort and Bean was a spy, that is to say an Indian Spy, and he was thought to be a good Soldier and very Trusty. He was in two actions that I knowed of. One of the actions was fought at or near the mouth of Capteen betwen our Spys and the Indians and our people was Defeted and an Nomber killed. The other action that [I] knowed Bean to be in was at Bakers Station near the mouth of Fish Creek on the Ohio. He continued to be with parties that was hunting the Indians of [off] an on untill the Indian war closed at Wayne's Treety and further this Deponent saith not. Sworn to and Subscribed before me the 8th day of November 1832.
Mitchel Atkinson, Justice of the peace

           John Daley (his mark)

John Shoptaw

 John Shoptaw submitted his claim for a pension from Bullitt County, Kentucky. With the application he included his deposition taken on September 17, 1832, a portion of which is transcribed below. The application was rejected because Shoptaw's service was well after the Revolutionary War.

 Shoptaw is the only participant to list Henry Enoch, Jr., as one of the company officers. He verifies Martin Baker's statement that "Shoptaw swam across the Ohio and escaped" and confirms that two of the scouts serving with him—Adam Miller and Isaac McKeown—were killed by Indians, and he stated that John Daniels was killed, also. This indicates that following the battle the men supposed Daniels to have been killed and did not *learn differently until Daniels later returned from captivity. By that time, Shoptaw was in Kentucky and never heard the news.*

In March 1791 James Marshel wrote to Colonel Shepherd to inform him that Ranger companies had been deployed to Fish Creek and Mill Creek. Shoptaw reports that he volunteered the first of March and that his company went to Fish Creek; another company under Captain Forbis was stationed thirty-five miles up the Ohio. Although the distance is not quite right this may be the company sent to Mill Creek; Captain Forbis may be Hugh Forbes of Somerset Township, Washington County, who served as a lieutenant in Captain Thomas Rankin's company on Crawford's Sandusky expedition in 1782.[151]

John's brother, William Shoptaw, submitted a supporting deposition which includes the following statement: "He was also well acquainted with said John Shoptaws officers." This indicates that the Shoptaws knew the Enochs—Henry, William and Abraham.

John Shoptaw pension application, Pennsylvania, O.W. Inv. Rej. 21684.

State of Kentucky
Bullitt County

On the 17th day of September 1832 Personally appeared in open Court before the Justices of Bullitt County now sitting, John Shoptaw, a Resident of said County of Bullitt and state of Kentucky aged sixty seven on the 1st day of March 1832 who being first duly sworn according to law doth on his oath make the following Declaration in order to obtain the benefit of the act of Congress passed June 7th 1832.

That he entered the service of the United States under the following named officers and served as herein stated, towit. About the 1st day of August 1788 a militia Company was ordered from the County of Washington in the state of Pennsylvania to guard the frontiers from Indian depredations. Said Company was

Commanded by a Captain Jenkins, Lieutenant Peter Drake, the name of the ensign not recollected and said John Shoptaw entered said Company as a substitute for Thomas Nichols.[152] The said Company rendesvouzed at a place called Lindley's mill in said County and thence marched about seventy miles to the Frontiers and he was appointed by Captain Jenkins as a spy. He performed his duty as such for one month and one week when said Company was relieved by another Company and he was discharged and returned home. He obtained no written discharge.

About the 1st day of March 1791 a Company of Pennsylvania militia was ordered from said County of Washington for the protection of the Frontiers and he volunteered in said Company. The officers of said Company was Captain Henry Enochs, Lieutenant William Enochs and Ensign Abraham Enochs. The Company rendesvouzed at the Town of Washington, County of Washington, Pennsylvania and Colonel Marshall of the Washington County militia appointed him and Isaac McKeown, John Daniels and Adam Miller spies. They were sworn by Colonel Marshall and he as the Commander of the spies received written instructions from Colonel Marshall which required him to spy and give information to Captain Enochs and other Companies who might be stationed on the Frontiers. The said Company marched from the said Town of Washington about one hundred miles and were stationed at the mouth of Fish Creek on the Ohio River. There was another Company of militia under the Command of Captain Forbis stationed on the Ohio River about thirty five miles above Captain Enochs. There were no regular officers or soldiers stationed where they were. He was constantly engaged as a spy from the time the Company marched, for six months, during which time he and his spies had two skirmishes with the Indians. In the first of which the said Isaac McKeown, John Daniels and Adam Miller were killed and he made his Escape and swan the Ohio river and joined the troops. After the Expiration of six months the Company was marched back to the Town of Washing-

ton, Pennsylvania and there discharged by Colonel Marshall. . . .
Subscribed and sworn to the day and year aforesaid.

John Shoptaw

John Yoho

John Yoho was a witness to the incident at Baker's Fort where John Bain was wounded, the same incident reported by John Dailey. Yoho's version, like Dailey's, appears in a statement supporting John Bain's pension application. Yoho's deposition was taken the day after Dailey's. It is similar in some respects and identical in others. For example, both men recalled that the incident took place "the last of June or the first of July," 1791. Yoho recalled that John Bain was treated by Joseph Biggs. It is surprising that Biggs, who suffered disabling wounds in April at Kirkwood's cabin and was still being tended to by Dr. Absalom Baird in Washington County in October, would have been at Baker's Fort dressing the wounds of John Bain in late June or early July.

Draper MSS 6ZZ100.

State of Ohio
Monroe County

Personally appeared before me John Linn one of the associate judges of the Court of Common Please of the said County John Yoho who being sworn according to law Deposeth and saith that as near as he can recollect that in the last of June or first of July in the year one thousand seven hundred and ninety-one I was forted at Bakers Station on the Ohio River about one mile below the mouth of Captina on the Virginia side. I was drawing logs for the purpose of building a block house, and I heard several guns on the Ohio side. I went to the Fort, and I saw John Bane swiming and several guns fired at him by the Indians, and he continued

swiming and a man by the name of Tate got in a Canoe to go to his assistance but returned without going to him. Then I seen the said John Bane carried to the Station and his wounds dressed by Joseph Biggs. The left thigh was badly wounded, and the right one slightly, and as near as I can recollect the said Bane was in service of the United States, and had been sent across the river for the purpose to see if there was any Indians, as there was some people on the Ohio side at work and that the said Bane was under Captain Brock and continued until legally discharged. Sworn and subscribed before me the twentieth day of June one thousand eight hundred and thirty-two.
John Linn, Associate Judge

John Yoho (his mark)

John Bain

John Bain submitted the deposition below in support of his brother Daniel's pension application. It gives a bit of personal information and confirms that Daniel Bain was involved in the Captina affair in May 1791 and the incident at Baker's Fort two months later.

Daniel Bean, Revolutionary War pension application, Pennsylvania, W. 8124.

State of Ohio
Muskingum County
Personally appeared before me, John Bane, who being duly sworn according to law, deposeth and saith that we lived on ten mile [Creek] when I was a boy and Daniel Bane was in the United States service at Fort Atkinson. I cannot tell exactly how long ago but I am now sixty-one or sixty-two years of age as near as I can tell and Daniel Bane is six or seven years older than I am.

The record of our ages was burned when the Indians burnt the house.

The reason why I know he was in the service of the United States is because he sent an order by me to Major McConnel for some of his pay and I got it for him. I am knowing that Daniel Bane was in the service nearly all the time untill General Wayne's treaty. I know of Daniel Bane being in the battle at Captine and when Baker's fort was attacked at or near the mouth of fish Creek on the Ohio River. Further this deponent saith not. Sworn and subcribed this 10th day of November 1832.
John Hammond, Justice of the Peace

John Bane (his mark)

Daniel Bain

Daniel Bain and his brother John were both participants in the battle of Captina. Daniel's statement in his pension application gives some personal information but only brief mention of his participation at Captina. He was stationed one summer at Atkinson's Fort, which was in Franklin Township and near where the Bain family lived in Strabane Township, Washington County. He also mentions serving at Ryerson's Station. Both Daniel and his younger brother, John, served under "Captain" Enoch.

Daniel Bean, Revolutionary War pension application, Pennsylvania, W. 8124.

State of Ohio
Muskingum County

On this 30th day of July 1833 Personly appeared in open Court before the Honourable Alexander Hasper, President Judge and his associate Judges for the County afforesaid Daniel Bean a resident of Brush creek Township in Muskingum County and

State of Ohio aged Sixty eight or nine year old as near as he can tell. I think I was Born in the month of March in the year one thousand Seven hundred and Sixty three or four, who first being Duly sworn according to Law doth on his oath make the following decliration in order to obtain the Bennefit of the act of Congress passed June 7th 1832.

That he Entered the Servis of the United States as an Indian Spy under the Command of Captain Reason Virgin in the Spring of the year 1781 and Served with him at Virgins Block house or Station During the whole Summer Season, being six or Eight months. The next Spring I think in the month of April I Inlisted in the United States Servis under the Command of Captain Charles Craycraft as a privet who was after that promoted to a major [i.e., Craycraft]. I Served Six months with him as an Indian Spy. This Servis was performed in the year 1782 being the Summer Crofford [Crawford] was Defeted. We was Stationed at Atkinsons fort. It is now in Washington County in Pennsylvania on a Creek called ten mile. The next Spring I think in March 1783 I Inlisted in the United States Servis under the command of Captain Blakeney as a privet at Riersons Station on Wheelein in Pennsylvania, also in Washington County. I Served Six months with him as an Indian Spy. This year peace was made with Great Britton but the war did not End with the Indians. I Continued to Serve evry Season, mor or less, as a Spy under Differat officers down to Waynes Trety with the Indians. While I was under the command of Captains Virgin, Craycraft and Blakney the Ground we used to Travel over to Spy out Indians was on the water of ten mile, Weelin, Fish Creek, Grave Crick and the Ohio. Captain Blakeney I thin was after ward promoted to a Collonel and resided at Washington. We was on the Frontiers and I did not know the field officers, if there was any. Being young, I do not remember them. I have no Discharge. The officers would tell us when our times ware out and Discharge us in that way.

I was in two actions. One at or near the mout of Captean. Captain Enoch was slain and an Nomber more with him. I allso was in the action at Bakers Station at the mouth of Fish Crick when the fort was besieged. Both of the actions was faut I think after the Revolution.

He hereby relinquishes every claim whatever to a pension or annuity Except the present and Declares that his name is not on the Pension Roll of the Agency of any State whatever. Sworn to and Subscribed the day and year afforesaid.

Daniel Bean (his mark)

John McDonald

John McDonald (1775-1853) was born in Northumberland County, Pennsylvania. His father moved west several times with the family—first to the site of present-day Steubenville, Ohio, and then to Washington, Kentucky—so that John spent all of his youth on the frontier. He served in the militia with Simon Kenton and in 1792 moved to Nathaniel Massie's station (now Manchester, Ohio). He became actively involved with Massie's surveying activities in Ohio and, with Massie, was one of the first settlers of Ross County. McDonald was a scout with General Wayne's army in 1794, and he rose to rank of colonel serving in the War of 1812.[153]

McDonald was in a position to present a very authentic account of the battle of Captina—he authored a biography of one the participants, Duncan McArthur, who was his brother-in-law. Both made their homes in Ross County. McDonald, writing in 1834, benefited from McArthur's first-hand recollections. According to McDonald:

> *Having been an humble actor in many of the scenes described, the incidents which I did not witness were communicated by the actors shortly after the events took place, so that the reader can place the fullest reliance in the truth of the narratives.*[154]

This account would be listed as Duncan McArthur's except for the fact that McDonald included certain details which he ob-

tained from other sources (e.g., Charley Wilkey's comments). While the bulk of the biography deals with McArthur's role in the War of 1812, McDonald does present a few of McArthur's frontier adventures, including the battle of Captina. Several of the dates, although close, are clearly wrong. He has McArthur commissioned an officer in 1791 and puts Captina in 1792, with McArthur a private. There is no question the battle occurred in 1791. McArthur is listed on a pay roll for July 1792 as an ensign in Captain Hercules Roney's militia company, and in November 1792 McArthur was listed as an ensign on a return of officers submitted to Governor Mifflin.[155]

McDonald is the only reporter on Captina to name an Indian participant—Charley Wilkey.

John McDonald, *Biographical Sketches of General Nathaniel Massie, General Duncan McArthur, Captain William Wells and General Simon Kenton* (Cincinnati, 1838), pp. 77-80.

The energy of McArthur's character began to unfold itself in very early life. No danger could appal him, nor fatigue deter him from the pursuit of an enterprise. Let us trace his early history.

In 1791, he was elected an ensign in a company of militia, and received his commission from Governor Mifflin, of Pennsylvania. Every militia officer in those trying times was expected to be shortly called upon to take his station in the "tented field." Consequently, the citizens were generally careful to select the best men the country afforded. There is no doubt that young McArthur felt more elated at that time, with an ensign's commission in his pocket, than he did in after life, when he was elected governor of Ohio.

In 1792, he joined, as a private, a volunteer company commanded by Captain William Enoch. This company was stationed at Baker's fort, on the river Ohio, some distance below Wheeling. A younger brother of Captain Enoch was lieutenant of the company. Shortly after their encamping on the river, and at a late hour in the evening, a few Indians were discovered across the river from the fort, on the Ohio shore, carelessly walking about. There is no doubt but these Indians showed themselves for the purpose of inviting the whites across the river, and if they could succeed, intended to lay in ambush and destroy them. Early the next morning Lieutenant Enoch with fifteen men, amongst whom was McArthur, crossed the river before day. As soon as it was light enough to distinguish objects at a distance, Lieutenant Enoch and his party went to the place where the Indians had showed themselves the previous evening, and found the trail of five or six Indians, and incautiously pursued them over the river hill to Captina creek, about one mile from the river, and not much further from the mouth of the creek. As the party of whites were pursuing the trail, they went down a small drain, with a narrow bottom. On the right of the drain was a steep, rocky bank, fifty of sixty feet high; on this bank thirty or forty Indians lay concealed. The whites passed on till they came in front of the Indian line, when a tremendous fire was opened upon them; the fire was instantly returned by Enoch and his party. Both parties took shelter behind trees, logs, or rocks, and the battle was continued with animation on both sides for some time. Lieutenant Enoch and McArthur were treed near each other, and loaded and shot several times. The hills along Captina creek are steep, high, and craggy, the valleys narrow, so that the keen crack of the rifles, added to the deafening shouts of the combatants, causing the echo to vibrate from hill to hill, made it seem that those engaged in this strife of arms were fourfold the actual number. At length a ball from an Indian's rifle pierced the breast of the brave Lieutenant Enoch; he fell, and immediately expired. Six others of his little band were slain, and some badly wounded.

Their commander being killed, and many of their gallant little band being slain or disabled, the remainder determined upon a retreat. No officer was left to command, and although McArthur was the youngest man in the company, in this time of peril he was unanimously called to direct the retreat. The wounded who were able to walk were placed in front, whilst McArthur, with his

Spartan band, covered the retreat. The moment an Indian showed himself in pursuit he was fired upon, and generally, it is believed, with effect. The Indians were so severely handled in the fight, that they soon gave up the pursuit. The same day the remains of the brave Lieutenant Enoch's command returned to Baker's fort, the place from which they set out in the morning.

In this engagement, McArthur had several fair shots; a man of his steady nerve would not often miss his mark. The Indians were commanded in this battle by a Shawnee chief, known to the whites about Chillicothe by the name of Charley Wilkey, (the same who took Samuel Davis prisoner). He told the author of this narrative, that the battle of Captina was the most severe conflict he ever witnessed; that although he had the advantage of the ground and the first fire, he lost the most men, half of them having been either killed or wounded. The carnage was indeed most fearful, considering the small numbers engaged. More than one half of each party were killed or wounded. I have never seen in print any account of this severe conflict with the savage foe.

McArthur's intrepid conduct in the Captina affair rendered him very popular with the frontier men, as far as the account of this sanguinary conflict extended.

George McKiernan

George S. McKiernan (1818-1887) was a collector of pioneer history and sometime author. He had several articles published in John S. Williams's American Pioneer, *a short-lived magazine devoted to western history and the frontier wars. Lyman Draper corresponded with McKiernan's widow in New Albany, Indiana, and learned that McKiernan's papers had not been saved.[156] Thus, the sources for this account are unknown. McKiernan gave this brief account in a letter to Williams:*

> *I have always been a sort of enthusiast in the study of border history. During a twelve years residence at Wheeling, I collected a mass of facts from manuscript*

> papers, and oral narrations, that will enable me in time to come, to furnish a goodly lot of scraps for the "Pioneer," if you think they would prove acceptable. . . .[157]

In the same letter, dated January, 13, 1843, McKiernan enclosed his account of the battle of Captina. At the end of the account he added this poignant note to Williams:

> The manuscript is badly written, as is this letter, but I am writing in a room without fire, and my fingers are benumbed with cold.

McKiernan's informants are unknown. He attributed most of his information to an "aged couple" who lived "in the valley of the Ohio."

George S. McKiernan, "Battle of Captina. A Scrap of Border History," *American Pioneer*, 2 (1843), pp. 176-179.

About the year 1782, the inhabitants of Fish-creek settlement, then in Ohio county, Virginia, erected a stockade work on the eastern bank of the Ohio river, at what is now called the head of Cresap's bottom. This post, which was known by the name of Baker's station, covered a space of about a quarter of an acre, and consisted of several block-houses connected by lines of stout pickets. Erected by the joint labors of the neighboring settlers, as a place of common refuge and security, whenever the Indians gave token of hostile designs, it was never regarded by the government as a place of sufficient importance to justify the maintenance there of a regular garrison; and when the presence of the enemy in the vicinity, caused the station to be the abiding place of the people, its garrison was composed of all persons within the enclosure; among whom might justly be included the wives and daughters of the frontier's-men, as they often stepped forward in the hour of danger, and rendered services of the most meritorious character.

A short time since, it was my good fortune to spend a few hours with an aged couple whose residence in the valley of the Ohio, commenced as far back as the "Indian war of the Revolution." From them I received the following narrative of an interesting event in border history, which I do not remember to have seen recorded in any of the chronicles of Indian warfare. The precise period at which it occurred has escaped their memory; but from their reference to contemporary events, which are yet fresh in their recollection, it probably took place in the year 1791.

Sometime in the spring of the year, rumors of a meditated attack upon the settlement, caused the people to concentrate, for safety, at Baker's station. A party of experienced scouts, consisting of John McDonald (or McDannel), Isaac McKeon, — Shopto and — Miller, crossed the river at the mouth of Captina creek, about a mile above the station, with the view of procuring some intelligence of the enemy's movements. They proceeded a short distance up the left bank of the creek, when a heavy fire was opened upon them by some Indians, who were concealed in a neighboring copse of undergrowth. Miller was killed on the spot, and McDonald, receiving a severe wound in the shoulder, soon became so much weakened by the loss of blood, that he was taken prisoner. McKeon and Shopto ran for their canoe at the mouth of the creek; but being closely pursued by the enemy, they continued their retreat down the bank of the river, with the hope of being able to distance the Indians. The latter, however, gained so much upon the fugitives, that they shot down McKeon on the beach immediately opposite the station; and Shopto, as a final resort, threw himself into the water, and was fortunate enough to swim to the station unharmed by the shower of balls that fell around him.

As soon as Shopto related his story, lieutenant Abraham Enochs (a militia officer from a distant part of the county, who happened then to be on a visit to Baker's station), proposed raising a party to march in pursuit of the Indians, and avenge the death of their three fellow-citizens. All the able-bodied men at the post—sixteen in number—promptly volunteered for the service; and, without loss of time, marched up the bank, and crossed over opposite the mouth of Captina. Shopto, together with three infirm old men, and the women and children, remained in the stockade, with instructions to keep themselves within the enclosure, until the return of the expedition.

Enochs' party, after proceeding about a mile up the creek, diverged from the course of the stream, crossed a heavily timbered ridge, and fell upon a small spring branch, about three quarters of a mile above its mouth. At this point, they were suddenly fired upon by the savages, who had formed an ambuscade in a bunch of dog-wood trees, covered with grape vines, that grew at a little distance from the run. The men were thrown into confusion at this unexpected attack; but Enochs, who is represented to have acted with admirable coolness, succeeded in restoring them to something like order; and, judging that the Indians might be dislodged from their position by making a prompt charge into the thicket, gave an order to that effect, but before the movement could be effected, that gallant officer received a shot in his heart, and fell lifeless to the ground. The enemy, encouraged at this circumstance, poured out a volley upon the whites, and then unmasking themselves , rushed out with a loud yell, brandishing their tomahawks above their heads. At the same instant, a second party of Indians, stationed about forty paces down the river, under cover of a thicket, opened a fire, which killed John Baker and a man named Hoffman, besides wounding three others. The men being now without a leader, and seized with consternation at discovering the infinite superiority of the foe, gave one fire, and then made a precipitate and disorderly retreat. Some went down the river, while others made the best of their way to the flats of Grave creek, and not one of them returned to Baker's station until the following day.

In the course of the night, the families that occupied the station, apprehending that lieutenant Enochs' party had been cut to pieces by the savages, deserted the stockade, and retreated for better security to the hills at the head of the bottom, where they concealed themselves until next day, when most of the fugitives from the battle, together with a strong party of men from Grave creek, arrived at the post. In the afternoon they crossed over to the scene of action, and recovered the bodies of Enochs, Baker and Hoffman, together with the three who had been killed before the battle. The remains of these unfortunate men were interred in a beautiful little grove near the station, and their graves are to be seen even at the present day.

Of the individuals engaged in the rencounter at Captina, besides Enoch, Baker and Hoffman, my informant can recollect only the names of George McColloch, Daniel Bean, John Sutherland and — Dobbins.

The Indians, agreeably to their custom, had scalped the men who perished in the combat, and stripped their bodies of every thing that seemed valuable. Whatever loss they sustained themselves, could only be estimated by conjecture. From the appearance of blood upon the leaves, and various indications of death-struggles on the ground occupied by the Indians, it was thought their loss amounted to seven or eight; notwithstanding the whites gave but a single fire, and even that at the moment of their greatest confusion.

Samuel Tomlinson

Samuel Tomlinson (1779-1846) was the son of Grave Creek pioneer, Joseph Tomlinson. Joseph and his brother Samuel settled on the flats at the mouth of Grave Creek in 1770. They built a cabin about a quarter of a mile from the Ohio River, near a group of ancient Indian mounds. With the onset of war in 1774, the Zanes built a fort at Wheeling and the Tomlinsons built one at Grave Creek. The Tomlinsons left their fort just before the Indians attacked Wheeling in the summer of 1777. Joseph took his family to Pike Run on the Monongahela. Joseph's brother, Samuel, was killed by Indians during the siege at

Fort Henry. The Indians burned the Tomlinsons' fort after the Foreman massacre at Grave Creek Narrows. About 1784 Joseph returned to Grave Creek with his family (including his young son, Samuel) and rebuilt the fort. Several years later, Dillie's Fort was built just across the river from the mouth of Grave Creek, and Baker's Station was built about eight miles downstream.[158]

Abelard Tomlinson, born in 1805, was Joseph's grandson. Abelard published his father Samuel's account of the Captina affair in John Williams's *American Pioneer*. It was part of a longer article on the history of the Grave Creek settlement, which later became Elizabethtown and is now Moundsville, West Virginia. The account opens, "My father, Joseph Tomlinson, was married near Cumberland, in the state of Maryland" and goes on to declare "I was born April 3rd, 1779." In a letter Abelard sent to the editor accompanying his history, he explained that his father was the narrator of the first-person account:

> I have succeeded in procuring for you a short narrative of the first settling of the Grave creek flat and neighborhood, but I fear it will be of but little consequence to you, owing to its being so destitute of correct dates. It is related by my father, whose memory is not capable, at this time [1843], of calling the dates to recollection; but if you will be able to use it, I will be gratified in considering that I have thus far contributed my mite of western incident. . . .[159]

Since the father's memory was called into question, the account which follows might be partly attributable to Abelard, rather than Samuel. Abelard may have done some "filling in" of details. The account is listed here as Samuel's, because Abelard stated that "it is related by my father."

Samuel Tomlinson was not a participant at Captina, so his account of the battle must be second hand. He was present when some of the survivors came straggling into the fort at Grave

Creek and would have heard reports of the action. Living that close to Baker's, he would have become acquainted with the details as they were recalled after the battle. At the time of the battle, however, he was only twelve years old. It is unfortunate that his account was not recorded until many years later. Abelard and Samuel Tomlinson achieved some notoriety in 1843, when they excavated "Mammoth Mound" at Grave Creek—the largest Adena burial mound in the U.S.[160]

A. B. Tomlinson, "First Settlement of Grave Creek," *American Pioneer, 1* (1843), pp. 353-354.

From this place [Baker's Station], John Bean and another person, as spies, crossed to the west side of the river. They had not proceeded far before they discovered two Indians, who saw them at the same time. Bean and his comrade retreated towards the river. Having arrived at the shore some time before the Indians, they were anxiously waiting an opportunity to give those at the fort signal for a craft, fearing to call aloud lest the Indians should the more easily find them. Whilst thus secreted under the bank of the river, the Indians approached. Bean and his comrade sprang into the river to escape to the other side by swimming. Bean received a slight wound in his thigh; his comrade was shot dead at the water's edge and scalped. Bean, by assistance from the fort, succeeded in reaching the other shore without further injury. Preparation was immediately made to go in pursuit of the Indians.

Those in the fort, fifteen or twenty in number, with captain Enochs at their head, crossed the river, and soon fell upon the trail of the two Indians. Their trail was pursued but a short distance, when it was discovered that they had fallen in with many others. Captain Enochs was induced to believe by the signs manifested, that the strength of the Indians was equal to his own. They [the Indians], however, followed on the trail, which soon fell upon Captina creek and proceeded up it, apparently marching along in a careless and deliberate manner, which induced captain Enochs and his men to believe that the Indians had not suspected the pursuit. After following the trail to the distance of about two miles from the river, they came to an Indian field, or prairie, as called by some. They struck the field about midway and proceeded through it. Captain Enochs had arrived at about the centre, when a galling fire was opened upon them from the west side of the field, from which no injury was sustained. A retreat was ordered to the other side, where a position was gained equal to the one occupied by the Indians, when a warm skirmish ensued until captain Enochs fell, when his men precipitately retreated toward the fort at Grave creek.

In the retreat, John Baker received a shot in his thigh and fell. Downing was behind Baker at the time and running in the same direction; as he came up to Baker he caught him up and set him on his feet, but he could not stand. Downing, seeing that no further assistance could be rendered to Baker, and being closely pursued by the Indians, again took to flight. George McCollough, whilst retreating in the advance, sprained ancle, which impeded his progress very much. Discovering that he must inevitably be caught if he did not seek a hiding place before discovered by the Indians, he turned on one side a few steps to a pool of water in a ravine, and sunk himself in it near the side of a log that lay there. Here he remained and distinctly heard those of his companions who were behind pass him, and soon after he heard the Indians also pass. When he heard the Indians pass back, he crept from the pool and proceeded on to Grave creek. During the same night they all arrived at the fort at Grave creek except Mr. McCollough, who arrived about ten o'clock the next day. In this ambuscade, captain Enochs and a Dutchman were killed on the ground, and Baker was found dead where seen by Downing. The number of Indians killed could not be ascertained, but signs where three had lain on the ground was distinctly seen. A sheaf of arrows, a bow, and a weasle skin full of red vermillion paint was also found upon the ground the next day when they had repaired there to bury the dead. It was discovered that the Indians had passed through the field to the opposite side, where they had turned short around, and marched back and secreted themselves near the edge of the woods, from whence the whites received the first fire.

William Harrod, Jr.

William Harrod, Jr., (1773-1847) belonged to a well-known pioneer family, which had many prominent participants in the Indian wars. His uncle, James Harrod, was the founder of Harrodsburg—Kentucky's first settlement (1774)—and a colonel in the militia. The military service of Colonel William Harrod, Sr., spanned a period of nearly forty years—from the French and Indian War through the end of the border wars in 1794. Many of the Harrod clan moved to the Tenmile Country in about 1765. William, Jr., grew up on his father's plantation on Tenmile Creek, located partly within the present-day town of Jefferson in Greene County. They were neighbors of the Enochs, who lived about three miles north at the forks of Tenmile Creek, near Clarksville. William, Jr., was a Ranger during the border war; he is on the roll for Abner Braddock's company in 1791 and for William Crawford's company in 1793.[161]

Harrod gave his account of the battle and the surrounding circumstances in an interview with Lyman Draper in November of 1845. His account appears to be based upon his own recollections of events—events with which he would have been familiar. He was eighteen years old at the time of Captina and already serving in the militia himself. However, since he was not present at the action, his version of the episode is necessarily second hand and was not given until fifty-four years after it occurred. His is the only account to place the battle of Captina immediately following the massacre of the Crow sisters. Harrod states from first-hand knowledge that William Enoch was a son of the Henry Enoch who had a fort at the forks of Tenmile Creek.

Draper MSS 37J171-172.

In April 1793, Colonel William Harrod lost his wife. About that time commanded a blockhouse high up on Wheeling Creek, some twenty-two miles. Commanded at Fish Creek a while.

While Harrod was at the blockhouse up Wheeling in spring of 1793, perhaps in May, Captain William Enochs with a party of men pursued Indians that had killed two of the widow Crow's daughters. About seven miles up Captina, they fell in with the enemy, and a battle ensued. Captain Enochs killed one Indian. Abraham McCoun killed another. The whites were defeated with the loss of Abraham and Isaac McCoun, Abraham Enochs, and (probably John) Lines, and perhaps more. Duncan McArthur was in this defeat. When a party returned subsequently, the body of Abraham Enochs (who was the first who was killed in the fight, being in the advance) was found cut up and mangled. The body of one of the McCouns was not found. Harrod had cautioned Captain Enochs not to follow much over the river.

Jackson's Fort on South Fork of Ten Mile was a principal station in that region. Ross', John Ancrim's on the South Fork of 10 [Mile], Jacob Kline on Muddy, John Van Metre's on Muddy, Legg's on Dunkard, William Miner's on Big Whiteley, Guthrie's on Big Whitely, John Swan's on Swan's run, Henry Van Metre's also on Swan's run, Henry Enoch's (father of Captain William Enochs) in the fork of the Ten Mile, Bell's on Rough Fork of Ten Mile and others.

Martin Baker

Martin Baker (1780-1857) was the son of John Baker, the Prussian immigrant who built the fort at Cresap Bottom and was killed by Indians near his fort in 1787. Martin became one of the early settlers of Monroe County, Ohio. He married Sarah Farnsworth in 1812—reportedly his second wife—and they had nine children. Baker lived just south of Woodsfield. He died in Monroe County and his will was probated there.[162]

The first printed version of Martin Baker's Captina account appeared in Henry Howe's Historical Collections of Ohio. Howe set out on horseback in 1846 to gather information for his book; during his tour of the state he visited 79 of Ohio's 83 counties. Describing his method, he explained that he "every where obtained information by conversation with early settlers and men of intelligence," in addition to making use of published sources and communications. Evidently, he interviewed Baker to obtain his story of the battle of Captina:

> Its incidents have often and variously been given. We here relate them as they fell from the lips of Martin Baker. . . .

Howe goes on to add that Martin was "at that time a lad of about twelve years of age in Baker's fort." Baker was actually only ten or eleven. Given his age at the time, some of his details may have been "borrowed" from others. He did get the date wrong, and as his account of Captina is the most familiar of all,[163] this error has caused much confusion.

Henry Howe, *Historical Collections of Ohio* (Cincinnati, 1847), pp. 55-56.

One mile below the mouth of Captina, on the Virginia shore, was Baker's fort, so named from my father. One morning, in May, 1794, four men were sent over according to the custom, to the Ohio side to reconnoitre. They were Adam Miller, John Daniels, Isaac McCowan, and John Shoptaw. Miller and Daniels took up stream, and the other two down. The upper scouts were soon attacked by Indians, and Miller killed; Daniels ran up Captina about three miles, but being weak from the loss of blood issuing from a wound in his arm, was taken prisoner, carried into captivity and subsequently released at the treaty of Greenville

[1795]. The lower scouts having discovered signs of the Indians, Shoptaw swam across the Ohio and escaped; but McGowan going up towards the canoe, was shot by Indians in ambush. Upon this, he ran down to the bank, and sprang into the water, pursued by the enemy, who overtook and scalped him. The firing being heard at the fort they beat up for volunteers. There were about fifty men in the fort. There being great reluctance among them to volunteer, my sister exclaimed, "She wouldn't be a coward." This aroused the pride of my brother, John Baker, who before had determined not to go. He joined the others, fourteen in number, including Captain Abram Enochs. They soon crossed the river, and went up Captina in single file, a distance of a mile and a half, following the Indian trail. The enemy had come back on their trails and were in ambush on the hillside awaiting their approach. When sufficiently near they fired on our people, but being on an elevated position, their balls passed harmless over them. The whites then treed. Some of the Indians came behind and shot Captain Enochs and Mr. Hoffman. Our people soon retreated, and the Indians pursued but a short distance. On their retreat my brother was shot in the hip. Determined to sell his life as dearly as possible, he drew off one side and secreted himself in a hollow with a rock at his back, offering no chance for the enemy to approach but in front. Shortly after, two guns were heard in quick succession; doubtless one of them was fired by my brother, and from the signs afterwards, it was supposed he had killed an Indian. The next day the men turned out and visited the spot. Enochs, Hoffman and John Baker, were found dead and scalped. Enoch's bowels were torn out, his eyes and those of Hoffman screwed out with a wiping stick. The dead were wrapped in white hickory bark, and brought over to the Virginia side, and buried in their bark coffins. There were about thirty Indians engaged in this action, and seven skeletons of their slain were found long after secreted in the crevices of rocks.

Daniel Wire

Daniel H. Wire (1798-1858) was a resident of Woodsfield in Monroe County, where he practiced law and served as the county prosecuting attorney. This brief addendum to the battle is taken from Wire's historical sketch of Monroe County. His account was published in Howe's Historical Collections of Ohio. *Wire, who appears to be speaking from first-hand knowledge, adds an interesting footnote to Captina.*

Henry Howe, *Historical Collections of Ohio* (Cincinnati, 1847), p. 367.

At the battle of Captina, John Baker was killed. He had borrowed Jack Bean's gun, which the Indians had taken. This gun was recaptured on the waters of Wills creek, about sixteen or eighteen miles west of Woodsfield, and still remains in the possession of some of the friends of the notorious Bean and the lamented Baker, in this county, as a memorial of those brave Indian fighters.

Wills de Hass

Wills de Hass (1817-1910) was a physician and anthropologist. He was born in Washington County, Pennsylvania, and after practicing medicine for a few years he moved to the panhandle area of what would later become West Virginia. There he pursued his interests in archeology and pioneer history. The Smithsonian Institute recognized de Hass's accomplishments by making him an associate of the Bureau of Ethnology.[164]
In the early to mid-eighteenth century, a number of writers produced histories of the trans-Allegheny settlement and the

Indian wars. One of the first was Alexander Withers's Chronicles of Border Warfare *in 1831. Another was de Hass's* History *in 1851. Although these histories made liberal use of oral tradition and suffer problems of reliability, de Hass made a significant effort to authenticate the information he received by interviewing and corresponding with aging pioneers.*

Fourteen individuals are named in de Hass's account, the most complete list of participants in the Captina affair. De Hass gives the name of only one of his informants, "the late venerable David McIntyre of Belmont County, Ohio, one of the most reliable and respectable men in the State." Abelard Tomlinson was likely another source; de Hass knew him well and was involved in the archeological studies which followed the opening of the Grave Creek mound. We can be sure that de Hass was also familiar with McKiernan's published account, as some passages are practically identical to McKiernan's.[165]

Wills de Hass, "1791, Affair at Captina, A Skirmish," in *History of the Early Settlement and Indian Wars of Western Virginia* (Wheeling, 1851, reprinted by McClain Printing Co., Parsons, WV, 1989), pp. 413-415.

One of the earliest settlers below Grave creek was John Baker. In 1775 he made an improvement on what is now known as Cresap's bottom. During the Dunmore war, Baker, with most of the settlers below Wheeling, resorted to the fort erected at that point; but in 1781, the settlement having become considerably strengthened by new additions, it was determined to erect a place of defence in the neighborhood, and accordingly, some additions were made to the house of Baker, and the whole protected by a stout stockade. Into this the settlers retreated on the renewal of hostilities in 1782.

Several years, however, passed without anything occurring at "Baker's Station," as it was called, worthy of special remark. At length, in 1791, an incident took place not unworthy of notice.

Indications of the enemy became manifest, and strong apprehensions began to be entertained that Indians were about. In order to satisfy themselves, five experienced hunters were sent over the river to scout. These were Isaac McKeon, John McDonald, John Bean, — Miller, and a Dutchman, named Shopto. They crossed opposite the station, and proceeded up to the mouth of Captina (one mile) and were moving cautiously along, when a heavy fire was opened upon them, killing Miller on the spot, and dangerously wounding McDonald, who was made prisoner. The others ran in the direction of the station, calling for help as they approached; and so close upon them were the Indians, that they shot McKeon after he had reached the beach opposite the fort. Shopto and Bean escaped by swimming.

Of the men collected at the station was Lieutenant Abraham Enochs, of the Ohio county militia, and he proposed at once to head a company and go in pursuit. Eighteen men, including all the efficient force of the station, at once joined the gallant officer, and at once left on their perilous duty. Shopto, Bean and four old men, were all the male adults left. These were ordered not to leave the fort until the expedition returned. Enochs led his men up the Virginia side to a point above the mouth of the creek, and then crossing the river, proceeded directly over the hill to the creek, instead of pursuing the bottom.

As the whole party were descending to a small stream which empties into the creek, about two miles above its mouth, they were fired upon by a large body of Indians, and John Baker (son of the proprietor of the station) severely wounded in the right thigh. The men were thrown into great confusion by this unexpected fire, and it was with the utmost difficulty they could be rallied. But Enochs, who possessed great intrepidity, as well as much tact as a commander, restored something like order, and cried to his men to rout the Indians from their covert. Leading them on with a shout of defiance, and a cry of confident victory, the bold and gallant officer, like Brunswick's fated chieftain, "Rushed to the field, and foremost, fighting fell." He received at the first onset a rifle ball in his breast, and fell dead on the spot.

The death of their leader, and a simultaneous outbreak of a new body of Indians, so disconcerted the rest of the men, that they gave but one fire, and then broke in a disordered and general rout, amid the shouts and terrible war-whoops of the savage. Every man retreated for himself, most of them making their way to Grave creek.

Of those wounded, was George McColloch, who received a rifle ball in his ancle. Ray Vennam one of the party, took him on his shoulder and carried him some distance, but McColloch, finding that they would be overtaken, entreated the other to take care of himself. Vennam concealed McColloch behind a log, and made his way to the fort. That night a man's plaintive cry was heard from the opposite shore, and on Vennam saying it was George McColloch, those in the fort said no, it was an Indian. Vennam, however, was firm in his opinion that it was his friend, and accordingly went over in a canoe to get McColloch. He [McColloch] had made his way that far on one foot.

On the following day a body of men from Grave creek, with most of the fugitives from the battle, went over to the scene of disaster. Baker, who had crawled under a rock, was dead, and, together with Enochs, scalped. Their remains, together with those who fell in the morning, were carried to the fort and decently interred. They lie in the rude burial place at the head of Cresap's bottom.

Of the men engaged in this affair, it is impossible to collect any other names than those of Enochs, Baker, McColloch, Hoffman, Bean, Sutherland, Dobbins, Vennam and McArthur. The latter, Duncan McArthur, afterwards Governor of Ohio, then a young man, had but recently gone to the station. He thus early evinced much of that true courage and great energy of mind and character which afterwards so distinguished him.

According to Mr. McIntyre, young McArthur cried out, as they ascended the bank, to "surround them," but the Indians having the advantage, spread themselves and would have prevented this even had the whites kept together.

Ezekiel Boggs

Ezekiel Boggs (1795-1866) was born near Wheeling and fought in the War of 1812. He was present at Detroit when General Hull surrendered to the British and Indians. Paroled and sent home, Ezekiel soon married Jane Neal and settled in Troy Township, Richland County, Ohio. In 1833 they moved to a farm near Lexington. Ezekiel was the son of Alexander Boggs, who was a participant in the Captina affair. Sometime in the 1850s Ezekiel was interviewed by Roeliff Brinkerhoff, a collector of the tales of Richland County pioneers. Ezekiel gave Brinkerhoff a brief account of the battle of Captina.

Roeliff Brinkerhoff (1828-1911) was born in New York and taught school in Tennessee, before finally settling in Richland County, Ohio, to practice law. He became the first to publish accounts of that county's pioneer settlers. From 1855 to 1859 Brinkerhoff was the editor and proprietor of the Mansfield Herald. *It was during this period that he began collecting and publishing the pioneers' stories in his paper. This enterprise was interrupted by the Civil War, which Brinkerhoff entered as a first lieutenant in 1861 and emerged as a brigadier general in 1866. After the war, he entered the banking business and continued to be active in numerous civic activities in Mansfield. The Ohio Archaeological and Historical Society was organized at his home in 1875, and he was its first president.*[166] *Brinkerhoff first came to Richland County in 1850, and speaking of that time stated that*

> Nearly twenty years ago, when many of the earlier settlers of Richland County were yet living, I commenced the collection of material for a pioneer history of Richland county, and nearly all that I have was gathered prior to 1861. My intention was to complete and publish in book form. The War, however, broke up all my calculations.[167]

Documentary Records

Brinkerhoff's work was collected and published in 1880 by A. A. Graham in Graham's History of Richland County.[168] *This publication appeared just after the American centennial and amid a whirlwind of publishing state and county histories. The book seems to have been hastily edited, and due to errors and omissions, the account of Captina is of little value. Fortunately, Mary Jane Henney has edited and published many of Brinkerhoff's original articles. The account below corroborates a number of details referred to by others and is the only one to place Alexander Boggs in the battle. Brinkerhoff's use of quotation marks indicates that he was relating the account in Ezekiel Boggs's words.*

Roeliff Brinkerhoff, *A Pioneer History of Richland County, Ohio*, Mary Jane Henney, editor (Mansfield, Ohio, 1993, reprinted from the *Mansfield Herald*, 1855-1859), pp. 338-339.

Ezekiel Bogs (Boggs) was born in Ohio County, Virginia, in the year 1795, near Wheeling. The father of Mr. Boggs [Alexander Boggs] was an early pioneer in Ohio, and was engaged in a battle with the Indians in Belmont County, which was fought along the shores of Captina Creek and which is thus described:

"About one mile below the mouth of Captina, on the Virginia side, was a small fort. A party of three or four scouts were sent out to reconnoiter and, being surprised by the Indians, were attacked, two of whom were killed, one taken prisoner and the other escaped. This aroused the vengeance of the fort, and a party of some twelve or fourteen soldiers crossed the river and marched up Captina in single file, when suddenly the report of the enemy rifles was heard on the brow of a hill above them, but the balls passed over their heads.

"The soldiers treed, and the skirmish commenced, in which three or four whites were killed and about ten of the enemy."

Jeremiah Hollister

Jeremiah Hollister (c1795-1867) lived most of his life in Woodsfield, Ohio. The town was laid out in 1812, and Hollister taught one of the first schools. As an associate judge of Monroe County, he helped Revolutionary War veterans file their applications for a pension under the act passed by Congress in 1832. Many of these men had served on the frontier.[169]

Hollister's account of Captina gives details of the scouting trip and the battle. The account dates from 1862, when, in the midst of the Civil War, he set down his version of the Captina affair in a series of letters to Lyman C. Draper of Wisconsin. His letter to Draper, dated February 22, states that

> I have thought some of giving you a short history of the Battle of Captina which was in Belmont County Ohio between seventeen white men and thirty Indians, but perhaps you have already obtained it. The whites were commanded by Lieutenant Abram Enochs who was killed.

He then sent Draper his account in a letter of March 1 and followed that with a letter on March 20 answering a number of questions posed in an intervening letter to him from Draper. In the March 20 letter Hollister drew a map showing the location of the battleground on Captina Creek.

Hollister lists a number of his informants, three of whom were participants—Martin Baker, John Daniels, and Daniel Bain. He probably knew John Bain, too, whom he refers to as "Jack Bean." In 1809, eighteen years after Captina, Hollister visited the battleground with Daniel Bain. At that time Hollister was living at the mouth of Captina Creek.

Hollister provides us with numerous details. Some are so explicit that we might tend to overlook the fact that his was second-hand knowledge, at best, and that his account was not set down until seventy years after the battle! In at least one instance, he may have inserted an unrelated event into his narrative: the McArthur "grape vine incident." Other authors—including McDonald, McArthur's biographer—put this incident at another place and time.[170] Hollister's letter of March 1 puts John Bain and a man named Tate over with the scouts on the first day (he has Tate being killed). In his letter of May 20, he corrects himself, writing that the spies who went over were as stated by Martin Baker.

Draper MSS 7E33, 34, 40.

[March 1, 1862] I will state some of the facts in relation of the fight with the Indians at Captina. I am not able to state the day of the month. It must have been in June 1791, for old John Daily was plowing corn. He had cleared about four acres immediately below the mouth of Captina Creek where the village of Powhatten now stands. He owned a negro man who was howing corn and his master Daily was plowing. This was on the Ohio side. There was a Block house about one mile below on the Virginia side caled Bakers Station. Four spies crossed the river on a scout: Jack Bean, John Daniels, — Tate, and the fourth I have forgot the name of. They were fired upon by about [thirty] Indians. One killed; John Daniels had his arm broke and was taken prisenor. Jack Bean and Tate reached the river. Tate threw off his shot pouch, hid his gun, and run to the river and was about to jump in when he was shot and fell in the river dead. Jack Bean swam the river and reached the Block house in safety and give the alarm and they sent a runner up and called over to Daily. He, having a horse and canoe, swam his horse over. Him and the colored man got safe to the fort. The Indians made their appearance opesite the fort and, being able to speak some Englis, hallowed over to the fort, repeating several times, "Turn out, turn out."

The next morning the men, seventeen in number, left the station to fight the Indians. Abraham Enochs, a regular officer of the united states army, having arrived the day before took the command and crossed the river. I can remember the names of John Baker, John (or Jack) Bean, Daniel Bean, Duncan McCarther and a McCullick. They followed the Indian trail about one mile up Captina Creek and crossed the creek to the north side to what was known as the cove, where the Indians were in ambush and the fight commenced—our men taking trees indian fashion—which lasted some time, when it was proposed by some of our men to run a few rods back up a hill, there being a thick cluster of small beach [beech] in the way between them and the enemy. They by so doing could shoot over the beach bushes. When the other men who had not heard the conversation seen them run, [they] supposed it to be a retreat and run also, and the panict became general and they could not be checked.

When they started to run they were exposed to the fire of the indians and Lietenant Abraham Enochs fell dead and John Baker fell mortally wounded. Two others were killed whose names I have forgotten. Baker was shot in the hips and drawed himself to a shelving rock where he hid, but the indians followed his trail and he had become to weak to shoot and was found tomahawked, scalped and his body dreadfully mutilated. In the race or retreat, McCarthur caut his foot in a grape vine and fell and several balls struck in the bank above and it was supposed his fall saved his life.

While the fight was going on the spy John Daniels, who had been taken prisenor the day before, was tied to a dogwood saplin on top of the hill, and one indian left with him with orders, if the indians were whiped, for the indian to tomahawk Daniels and run. If not, to loose him and join the company. Accordingly, Daniels was conducted down to the Battle ground where the indians buried or covered their dead with stone. There were seven indians killed and ware laid in a row and covered with a large pile of stone. Daniels afterwards somehow was released and returned to Baker's Station and related his story.

In the spring of 1809 I went with several others, Daniel Bean in company, to the Battle ground. The dead Indians had been uncovered but the heads or sculls all lay together, seven in number, and ware yet all sound. There is a brother of John Baker yet living near Calis [Calais], Monroe County, Ohio. His name is Jacob Baker. I have often heard Martin Baker relate the account of the Battel. He was in the Block house, a boy of twelve years old at the time. . . .

[May 20, 1862] In reply to yours of the 12th I will state that I can describe the locality of the Battle ground on Captina as I resided five years at the mouth of the said Captina Creek. The Ohio river at that place runs verry nearly a south course and the creek for about a half mile up from the mouth runs directly east and then makes a curve perhaps a forth of a circle. About one mile up on the north side of the creek is what is known as the cove. Two small runs or dreans come in to the creek two or three hundred yards apart and between these runs there is a low ridge where our men were led into ambush. The Indians had made a trail directly up the ridge and then fell back on each side in the ravines and waited the approach of our men. . . .

What ever became of Jack Bean I do not know. Daniel Bean removed to Muskingum County Ohio where he obtained a pension under the act June 7th 1832 and died there. As to John Daniels I have no knowledge but will refer you to Isaac Baker, brother of John Baker who was killed in the Battle of Captina. Isaac Baker is the youngest of the Baker family. There were George John Henry Jacob Martin and Isaac Mary and Elisabeth. Isaac was about ten years old at the time of the Battle of Captina and Lived in the Block house or Baker's Station. Jacob who resided on Wills Creek died Last fall. You will find this Isaac Baker now living with his son Jacob Baker in Taswell County, state of Illinois. Armington is his post office. I think he can tell what became of John Daniels and Jack Bean and give the history of Jack Beans gun. The story was that Jack Bean had two guns in the fort or station and that Bakers gun was out of order. If the tale of the recapture of this gun is true, Isaac Baker can tel it correctly. He was intimately acquainted with the circumstances.

I know nothing of those men you mention except John Sutherland. I was personally acquainted with his brother David Sutherland, but John I believe lived and died on Fish Creek Virginia.

On more mature reflection I am of opinion that the spies mentioned who went over the river the day before the Battle of Captina were as stated by M[artin] Baker....

I have learned further that Jack Bean when he left Captina settled on the big Buffalow fork of Wills Creek at a place now caled Cumberland. I believe in Morgan County Ohio.

Samuel Hedges

Samuel Hedges (c1783-) was born in what is now Brooke County, West Virginia, where his father, Joseph Hedges, settled in 1772. Joseph was the brother of Colonel Silas Hedges. The Hedgeses, of English descent, immigrated to New Castle County, Delaware, by 1702 and located on the Monocacy River in Maryland by 1730. From there, a number of the Hedgeses migrated to the area of Washington County, Pennsylvania, and the panhandle region of Virginia.

Samuel Hedges later moved to Cadiz, Harrison County, Ohio. He was residing there in the fall of 1863 when Lyman Draper stopped in to see him. Draper was on a tour of midwestern states collecting frontier materials and visiting with surviving pioneers. Draper recorded his lengthy interview with Hedges on October 7 and 8. The brief portion dealing with Captina names seven participants—George McColloch (with whom Hedges was acquainted), Shoptaw, McCowan, Daniel Bain, Enoch, Hoffman and John Baker. Hedges corroborates several details and provides a few new ones. His is the only account to mention that McColloch and Bain came to the aid of Shoptaw and that the Ranger company crossed the Ohio in two pirogues (large, canoe-like boats).[171]

Draper MSS 19S220-221.

Captina Battle—George McColloch, ahead mentioned, was in it. Indians ran spies in in the morning and Shoptaw and one McCune jumped into the river over [on the Ohio side] and McCune was shot and sank. McColloch and Daniel Bean went over from Baker's Station in a canoe and saved Shoptaw. Then upwards of twenty men gathered and went over in two pirogues under Captain Enochs, commanding at Baker's, his men mostly from Ten Mile. Saw a few Indians playing off at the back of the bottom, teased on the whites till they were surrounded. Enochs and two others killed, Hoffman one and John Baker, and got defeated. Daniel Bean lived near Blue Rock [Gaysport, Muskingum County] on Muskingum and was living not long since.

Frontier Rangers
1791

Few militia rolls for the year 1791 have survived. Records for Ohio County, Virginia, are better than for Washington County, Pennsylvania. The extant lists for each county are reproduced below. Original spelling is preserved. Duplicate names were deleted, and the lists were rearranged in alphabetical order. Rank was "private" unless stated otherwise.

Ohio County Militia

This list is taken from pay rolls in the David Shepherd Papers, which are part of the Draper Manuscripts.[172] The rolls are incomplete.

Allender, William
Andrews, James
Armstrong, Hugh
Athson, James
Barber, Henry
Barr, David
Barrett, John
Bell, Philip, Ens.
Berdeen, Nathan
Biggs, Joseph, Ens.
Bilderbeck, Thomas
Brown, Robert
Bruner, Michael
Cain, Abel
Caldwell, Samuel
Carson, Robert
Cochas, George
Conner, James
Conner, John
Coyle, William
Croghan, James
Cummins, James
Dailey, John
Darnald, Thomas
Darnald, Cornelius
Darnald, Henry
Davis, David
Davis, Jesse, Sgt.
Delong, Solomon
Demas, Jacob
Dement, William, Sgt.
Duncan, John
Edgenton, George
Edgenton, Isaac
Edgenton, John, Sgt.
Erelwine, John

Fordice, Samuel
German, William
Gray, Thomas
Grindstaff, Adam
Grist, John
Hall, John
Hedge, Elijah
Hedge, Joseph
Hendricks, David, Sgt.
Holms, Isaac, Sgt.
Holmes, Joseph
Irvin, William
Jolly, John
Jolly, William
Kellor, John
Kelly, John
Kerns, Mathew
Kirk, John, Sgt.
Lamasters, John
Lashley, Joseph
Lines, Simon
Lockwood, Benjamin, Ens.
Lucas, Benjamin
Martin, Elijah, Sgt.
McCulloch, George
Meek, Joshua
Mercer, George
Mills, Edward
Mills, Thomas
Morgan, John, Lt.
Morrison, William
Morton, Thomas
Murry, Michael
Patterson, Joel
Perry, Braden
Peyatt, Robert

Pollyard, Jonathan, Sr.
Purdie, Daniel
Rannels, Thomas
Rawlings, William
Richards, Thomas
Robinson, Israel, Sgt.
Scarmahorn, Joseph
Scott, James
Scoutchfield, Nathan, Sgt.
Scutchfield, William
Seaman, Jonah, Lt.
Shepherd, William
Skinner, Richard
Sloan, Joseph
Smith, Thomas
Smith, William, Sgt.
Spencer, John
Steenrod, Briggs, Sgt.
Tarol, Daniel
Taylor, John
Tucker, John
Tucker, William
Vanbuskirk, Laurence, Lt.
Vanmetre, Joseph
Walker, John
Warnock, Jacob
Warnock, John
Waxler, Michael
Whetsell, John
White, William
Williams, Charles
Williams, William, Sgt.
Williamson, Jeremiah
Williamson, Moses
Wilmoth or Welmeth, Francis
Wilmoth, Jeremiah

Wilson, Isaac
Wilson, John
Wood, Isaac

Woods, Edward
Woods, Joseph
Wright, Alexander

Washington County Militia

The *Pennsylvania Archives* contain 1791 pay rolls for two militia detachments—Sergeant Abner Braddock's (April-May) and Captain William Laughlin's (June)—and mention one other company—Captain Alexander Kidd's.[173] These names are only a small fraction of the those who served in 1791 from Washington County.

Aten, Curnelis
Bartholemen, John
Braddock, Abner, Sgt.
Chamberlan, Stout
Claffin, John
Copus, James
Cowhern, Joseph
Cowhern, William
Darrah, Joseph
Darrah, Robert
Davis, Jessie
Dawson, None
Eaten, James
Enock, Enock, Jr.
Ferrel, Thomas
Garrison, George
Glasgow, Stephen

Hall, Adam
Hearcey, William
Herrod, William
Jinkens, Joseph
Jones, Joseph
Jones, Meckle
Kidd, Alexander, Capt.
Laughlin, William, Capt.
McCoy, William
McGraw, Thomas
Patton, David, Capt.
Six, Philip
Stephens, Samuel
Stephenson, William
Whitehill, James
Williams, Hugh

Notes

[1] Tribes occupying the Northwest Territory in 1787 included the Delaware, Kickapoo, Mahican, Miami, Moravian, Munsee, Ojibwa (Chippewa), Ottawa, Potawatomi, Seneca, Shawnee, Wea and Wyandot (Huron). Richard White, *Middle Ground, Indians, Empires, and Republics in the Great Lakes Region, 1650-1815* (Cambridge, England, 1991), pp. 414-415.

[2] Richard White, *Middle Ground*, pp. 436-440, 443-448. These agreements included the treaties of Fort McIntosh (1785), Great Miami River (1786) and Fort Harmar (1788). U.S. Congress, *American State Papers, Indian Affairs, Volume 1 (Washington, DC, 1833)*, pp. 5-11.

The treaties called for peace and prohibited white occupation of Indian lands. The confederacy ignored the treaties, and even U.S. troops could not prevent white "squatters" from settling in Indian territory.

[3] Judge Harry Innis described the problem Kentucky had faced from the end of the Revolutionary War to 1790 in a letter to Secretary of War Henry Knox.

> Since my first visit to this district [in 1783], I can venture to say that fifteen hundred souls have been killed and taken in the district and migrating to it; that upwards of twenty thousand horses have been taken and carried off; and that other property, such as money, merchandise, household goods and wearing apparel, have been carried off and destroyed by these barbarians, to at least £15,000.

Bradford, *Notes on Kentucky*, in Thomas Clark, editor, *Voice of the Frontier*, (Lexington, KY, 1993), p. 134.

[4] Mary Cone, *Life of Rufus Putnam* (Cleveland, 1886), pp. 64-65. Rufus Putnam (1738-1824) grew up in Massachusetts and taught himself the art of surveying. As a young man he served in the French and Indian War and later in the Revolutionary War as a lieutenant-colonel. After the war, as the head of the Ohio Company, he arranged the purchase of 1.5 million acres of western land from the federal government. On April 7, 1788, his company settled Marietta—the first town in the Northwest Territory. He was appointed U.S. surveyor general (1796-1803) by President Washington and died at Marietta.

[5] Jacob Burnet, *Notes on the Early Settlement of the North-Western Territory* (New York, 1847), pp. 42-46. Columbia is five miles upstream from Cincinnati, North Bend is sixteen miles downstream. Stites, Denman and Symmes all came out from New Jersey. These settlements were located on a tract that was referred to as the Symmes Purchase.

John Cleve Symmes (1742-1814) was born on Long Island, New York. After fighting in the Revolution, he settled in New Jersey, where he became chief justice of the state and was elected to Congress. In 1788 Symmes contracted with the government to buy approximately one million acres in Ohio located between the Big Miami and Little Miami rivers. Although he sold much of this land, he came up short on being able to pay for it. Symmes eventually obtained a patent for 248,250 acres in 1794. The lands he sold beyond his patent had to be repurchased by the settlers from the federal government. Judge Symmes settled on his Ohio lands and built a mansion at North Bend. His daughter Anna married William Henry Harrison, who became the ninth President of the U.S. Beverly Bond, editor, *Correspondence of John Cleves Symmes* (New York, 1926).

Notes

The name "Losantiville" was chosen by John Filson (one of the first proprietors of Cincinnati and author of the first history of Kentucky). *L-os-anti-ville* stood for "town opposite the mouth" of the Licking River, which enters the Ohio from the Kentucky side at Cincinnati.

[6] Ironically, since the new settlements in Ohio were on U.S. soil, they were protected by U.S. troops stationed at Fort Harmar and Fort Washington. Marietta was built adjacent to Fort Harmar and Fort Washington was erected at Cincinnati in the fall of 1789.

[7] John Bradford, *Notes on Kentucky*, p. 133.

[8] Josiah Harmar (1753-1813), a native of Philadelphia, spent most of his life in the military. He served throughout the Revolutionary War and in 1784 was sent to France to represent the U.S. at the treaty signing. He was appointed Indian Agent of the Northwest Territory in 1785 and commissioned a brigadier general by Congress in 1789. After leaving the army, Harmar served as adjutant general of Pennsylvania for Governor Thomas Mifflin and was responsible for providing troops for the western frontier in 1793-94 and for western Pennsylvania during the "Whiskey Insurrection" in 1794. *Pennsylvania Archives, Series 2, Volume 4*, p. 115.

[9] I. D. Rupp, *Early History of Western Pennsylvania* (Laughlintown, PA, 1989, reprint of the 1847 edition), appendix, pp. 225-233.

[10] Alexander Withers, *Chronicles of Border Warfare* (Cincinnati, 1895), p. 395.

[11] Despite the public face put on for this campaign, the enormity of the defeat soon became apparent, and Harmar was relieved of duty by the Commander in Chief, George Washington. A year later, in September 1791 at Fort Washington, Ohio, a court of inquiry exonerated Harmar of charges of drunkenness and misconduct. U.S. Congress, *American State Papers, Military Affairs, Volume 1* (Washington, DC, 1832), pp. 20-36.

An able officer in the Revolutionary War, Harmar was deemed unfit for command on the frontier, where he demonstrated a lack of knowledge of Indian methods of warfare and an inability to deal with the militia. Harmar, however, maintained that fault for his defeat lay solely with the cowardice and insubordination of the militia. In a speech to both houses of Congress (October 25, 1791), President Washington made a point to distance himself from Harmar's opinion:

> Some of these [expeditions against the Indians] have been crowned with full success, and others are yet depending. The expeditions which have been completed, were carried on under the authority, and at the expense of the United States, by *the militia of Kentucky, whose enterprise, intrepidity, and good conduct, are entitled to peculiar commendation.* (emphasis added)

The campaign "yet depending" was General St. Clair's. On November 4, 1791, a week after the speech, St. Clair's army would be broken on the plains of the upper Wabash by the combined forces of Little Turtle and Blue Jacket. This battle is still considered to be the worst defeat ever suffered by an American army. U.S. Congress, *State Papers and Publick Documents of the United States, Volume 1* (Boston, 1817), pp. 22-23.

[12] Usually referred to as Little Turtle's War (1790-1795). The dates relate to Harmar's defeat in 1790 and the treaty of Greenville in 1795.

[13] Theodore Roosevelt, *Winning of the West, Volume 3* (New York, 1894), p. 310.

[14] Joseph Barker, *Recollections of the First Settlement of Ohio*, quoted in Emily Foster, editor, *Ohio Frontier, An Anthology of Early Writings* (Lexington, KY, 1996), pp. 88-94. Joseph Barker (1765-1843) and his wife Eliza left Massachusetts and settled at Marietta in 1789. He acquired a farm along the river and was also engaged in building houses and operating a shipyard. Barker built the home of the ill-fated Harmon Blennerhassett.

[15] Taken from the journal of Rufus Putnam, in Mary Cone, *Life of Rufus Putnam* (Cleveland, 1886), p. 67. Putnam, who personally kept George Washington informed of the Ohio Company's affairs at Marrieta, wrote to the president on January 8, 1791, describing the attack at Big Bottom. His letter began, "Sir, The mischief which I feared, has overtaken us much sooner than I expected." U.S. Congress, *American State Papers, Indian Affairs, Volume 1*, pp. 121-122.

Those killed at Big Bottom include John Stacey, Ezra Putnam, John Camp, Zebulon Groop, Jonathan Farwell, James Couch, William James, Joseph Clark, Isaac Meeks and his wife and two children. Francis Choat, Isaac Choat, Thomas Shaw, Philip Stacey and James Patten were taken prisoners. For other accounts of Big Bottom, see Henry Howe, *Historical Collections of Ohio, Volume 2* (Cincinnati, 1902, Centennial edition), pp. 303-305; Joseph Barker, *Recollections of the First Settlement of Ohio*, pp. 88-94; and T.W. Lewis, *Zanesville and Muskingum County, Volume 1* (Chicago, 1927), p. 51.

[16] Henry Howe, *Historical Collections of Ohio, Volume 2*, p. 800.

[17] James McBride, *Pioneer Biography, Sketches of the Lives of Some of the Early Settlers of Butler County, Ohio, Volume 1* (Cincinnati, 1869), appendix, pp. 87-88; "Attack of Dunlap's Station" *American Pioneer 2* (April 1843), pp. 148-149; *Cist's Weekly Advertiser* (Cincinnati), March 21, 1848. These accounts were provided by various participants—including William Wiseman, Samuel Hahn, Thomas Irvin and John Wallace—who recalled events somewhat differently. Wallace placed the event on January 8, while Wiseman put it in early February. Some said the Indians were led by a white man—Simon Girty—and one account put Little Turtle as the leader.

[18] Reverend John Shane interviews with Benjamin Stites, Joseph Martin and Levi Buckingham, Draper MSS 13CC66, 81, 89-93; letter from Itinerus to the *Daily Evening News*, November 5, 1845, in Draper MSS 26CC94.

[19] Letter from Dr. William Goforth to the *Cincinnati Chronicle*, September 3, 1791, in Draper MSS 19CC53.

[20] *Kentucky Gazette*, April 2, 1791; *Western Review 1* (1819), pp. 48-53; Bradford, *Notes on Kentucky*, pp. 139-144; Lewis Collins and Richard Collins, *History of Kentucky, Volume 2* (Frankfort, KY, 1966, reprint of 1874 edition), pp. 700-702; *Calendar of Virginia State Papers 5* (1885), p. 282.

[21] January 25, 1791, Draper MSS 3SS1.

[22] Draper MSS 2S195; 3SS137, 139. The hunters who were reported to have escaped include Joseph Biggs, James and Alexander Mitchell, Thomas Barr, Thomas Richards, Elijah Whittaker, and Joshua Williamson. Wills de Hass, *History of the*

Early Settlement and Indian Wars of Western Virginia (Wheeling, WV, 1851), pp. 316-317.

[23] David Shepherd to Thomas Mifflin, April 21, 1791, *Calendar of Virginia State Papers* 5 (1885), p. 289.

[24] Lyman Draper interview with Joseph Holmes, Draper MSS 19S185-186; Draper interview with Samuel Hedges, Draper MSS 19S200-202; Draper interview with Philip Bruner, Draper MSS 20S216, 223; J.A. Caldwell, *History of Belmont and Jefferson Counties, Ohio* (Wheeling, WV, 1880), p. 431. Ruth Schemerhorn was one of the Riley girls captured; they were traded to the Chippewa and later married French Canadians. Both declined to return to their family after Wayne's treaty. The infant girl killed at the cabin may have been Ruth's daughter. One of the sons killed was William Riley. The father, Francis Riley, was away from home at the time of the attack.

[25] Samuel Brady (1756-1795) was born in Shippensburg, Pennsylvania, and served in the Continental Army during the Revolutionary War. After his father was killed by Indians in 1779, Samuel swore a life long vengeance. He married Drusilla Swearingen in 1784, and they lived near Wellsburg in what was then Ohio County, Virginia. Samuel led a band of famed frontier scouts from after the Revolutionary War to the end of the border wars in 1794. Louise Kellogg, *Frontier Advance on the Upper Ohio, 1778-1779* (Madison, WI, 1916), pp. 158-159.

[26] Robert Woods dispatch, March 2, 1791, Draper MSS 3SS3.

[27] Thomas Mills (c1765-after 1834) was born in Maryland and lived at Wheeling during the Revolutionary War. He entered the militia in 1781 under Captain Silas Zane, and in 1782 he was

nearly killed during the second siege of Wheeling, receiving eight bullets wounds. Following his recovery, he served again in the militia and was with Joseph Biggs's Ranger company at Kirkwood's blockhouse. After peace was made, Mills resided in Tyler County, Virginia, and later moved to Monroe County, Ohio, to live with some of his children. Thomas Mills, Revolutionary War pension application, Virginia, S. 16200.

[28] Francis McGuire (c1754-1820) was a son of Thomas McGuire, an Irish emigrant, who came to Washington County, Pennsylvania, from the South Branch of the Potomac and settled near the head of Buffalo Creek. Francis served throughout the Revolutionary War and was on a number of western campaigns, including the Coshocton expedition. He sat on the first court held in Brooke County, Virginia, in 1797 and at the second session was selected as one of the commissioners. Francis, or Frank, was described by contemporaries as "a very heavy man." He is buried one-half mile west of Independence, Pennsylvania, very near the West Virginia state line. Rueben Thwaites and Louise Kellogg, editors, *Frontier Defense on the Upper Ohio, 1777-1778* (Madison, WI, 1912), p. 40; Draper MSS 20S121-126; Joseph Doddridge, *Notes on the Settlement and Indian Wars of the Western Parts of Virginia and Pennsylvania from 1763 to 1783* (Pittsburgh, 1824), p. 229.

[29] Cornplanter to George Washington, March 17, 1791, *Pennsylvania Archives, Series 2, Volume 4*, pp. 546-547. This action caused Brady and McGuire no end of grief, culminating sometime later with the governors of Virginia and Pennsylvania offering a reward for their arrest. Brady later stood trial in Allegheny County for murder and was acquitted. The case came before the Court of Oyez and Terminer on May 20, 1793, Chief Justice Thomas McKean presiding. The proceedings were reported in the *Pittsburgh Gazette*:

The only criminal business that came before the Judges was the trial of Captain Samuel Brady who, when the Judges were last here, had been indicted for murder, in killing certain Indians near the mouth of Beaver creek, in the spring of the year 1791. It was proved to the satisfaction of the court, that notwithstanding the treaties of Fort Stanwix, McIntosh, Muskingum, and Miami, which established peace between the Indians and the people of the United States and obliged the Indians to surrender up all who should commit any murder on our frontiers, certain banditti of them had from time to time infested the western frontier, stolen horses, taken boats, and murdered our citizens; that recently before the killing of the Indians, for which Brady was now tried, several people from Ohio county—particularly [James] Boggs, Paul, [Francis] Riley's family, and Mrs. [Lawrence] Vanbuskirke [i.e., Rebecca]—had been put to death; that to pursue the Indians who had committed these murders and to recover some of the property stolen, a party of volunteers from Ohio county, of which Brady was one, crossed the Ohio and led by the trail of the Indians towards the place where the killing happened, fired and killed those for whose death Brady was tried. It was proved by the oath of Kayashuta, an Indian chief, that the Delawares had long before let go the chain, that they, the Shawanese, Chippawas, Ottawas, Wyandots, and some renegade Mingoes, were in the battle against General Harmar in 1790. It was also proved that the attack and firing of Captain Kirkwood's house was by Delawares, that some of the instances of murder and rapine above mentioned were by Delawares, that the persons killed were Delawares, had in their possession some of the property just before taken from Ohio county, manifested an intention of proceeding to commit other murders on our citizens, and when fired on by those who attacked them, and whom they had just discovered, were in the act of seizing their guns; and moreover the relation of John Hamilton, a trader on the spot (which is hereto subjoined) satisfied the court of the malign and hostile temper of those very Indians.

The jury found Brady innocent of the charges without leaving the jury box. *Pittsburgh Gazette*, May 25, 1793.

[30] James Morrison to Richard Butler, March 17, 1791, *Pennsylvania Archives, Series 2, Volume 4*, p. 546.

[31] Zadok Cramer, *The Navigator, Containing Directions for Navigating the Monongahela, Allegheny, Ohio and Mississippi Rivers....* (Pittsburgh, 1814, 8th edition), pp. 76-78. This early publication for travelers on the Ohio River gives the location and description of all the tributaries, islands and settlements downstream from Pittsburgh.

[32] Presley Neville (1756-1818), a Revolutionary War veteran and the son of General John Neville, lived on a plantation on Chartiers Creek and had a home in Pittsburgh. While living in Allegheny County, he served as surveyor of the county, member of the General Assembly and brigade inspector of the militia. Presley and his father later played a prominent pro-government role in the Whiskey Rebellion. Clara Duer, *Pittsburgh Gazette Abstracts, 1786-1797*, pp. 6, 17, 137.

[33] Presley Neville to Richard Butler, March 25, 1791, *Pennsylvania Archives, Series 2, Volume 4*, pp. 548-549.

[34] John Wilkins, Jr. (1761-1816), was promoted to general in 1793 and appointed commander of all the militia forces in Allegheny County. John spent most of his career in the military,

beginning at age fifteen, when he enlisted as a surgeon's mate in the Revolutionary War. At the time of his death, he was quartermaster general of the U.S. army. His father was prominent in the civic affairs of early Pittsburgh. Clara Duer, *People and Times of Western Pennsylvania, Pittsburgh Gazette Abstracts, 1786-1797* (Pittsburgh, 1988), p. 21.

[35] John Wilkins, Jr., to Thomas Mifflin, March 31, 1791, *Pennsylvania Archives, Series 2, Volume 4*, pp. 551-552.

[36] In 1791, Ohio County, Virginia, included the present-day West Virginia counties of Hancock, Brooke, Ohio, Marshall, Wetzel, Tyler, Pleasants and Doddridge.

[37] Presley Neville to Richard Butler, March 25, 1791, *Pennsylvania Archives, Series 2, Volume 4*, pp. 548-549.

[38] James Marshel (c1749-1829) settled in Cross Creek Township, Washington County in about 1778 and was appointed county lieutenant in 1781. He served as a member of the State Convention that ratified the U.S. Constitution. Marshel lived for many years in Washington, the county seat; served as sheriff of the county and represented his district in the General Assembly. In 1795, he sold his land there and moved to Brooke County, Virginia. James Marshel obituary, *Pittsburgh Gazette*, copy in Draper MSS 27CC15; Boyd Crumrine, *History of Washington County, Pennsylvania* (Philadelphia, 1882), p. 728.

[39] James Marshel to Thomas Mifflin, February 19, 1791, *Pennsylvania Archives, Series 2, Volume 4*, pp. 538-539.

[40] David Redick (-1805) was one of the first residents of Washington. He was a native of Ireland, and after settling for a time in

Lancaster County, Pennsylvania, he moved to Washington County, where he was admitted to the bar in 1782. Redick was prominent in the early affairs of the county. He served on the Supreme Executive Council of Pennsylvania in 1786 and held numerous positions in Washington County, including surveyor, prothonotary and clerk of the court. Boyd Crumrine, *History of Washington County*, pp. 476-479.

[41] David Redick to Thomas Mifflin, February 20, 1791, *Pennsylvania Archives, Series 2, Volume 4*, p. 540.

[42] Henry Knox to the western county lieutenants, March 3, 1791, Draper MSS 3SS5-7.

[43] Samuel Shepard to Beverly Randolph (enclosure from R.J. Vanden Broek), April 30, 1790, *Calendar of Virginia State Papers 5* (1885), p. 146.

[44] Henry Knox to the western county lieutenants, March 10, 1791, Draper MSS 3SS9-11.

[45] Peter Boyd, *History of Northern West Virginia Panhandle, Volume 1* (Topeka, IA, 1927), p. 169.

[46] Francis Parkman, *Conspiracy of Pontiac, Volume 2* (Boston, 1875, 8th edition), pp. 115-116.

[47] James Marshel to David Shepherd, March 23, 1791, Draper MSS 3SS19.

[48] John Shoptaw, Revolutionary War pension application, Pennsylvania, O.W. Rej. 21684. Captain Henry Enoch, Jr.'s company

included William Enoch, lieutenant; and Abraham Enoch, ensign. "Captain Forbis" was probably Hugh Forbes of Washington County, who was on the tax list for Somerset Township in 1781 ("Effective Supply Tax for the County of Washington," *Pennsylvania Archives, Series 3, Volume 14*, p. 770). Forbes had previous officer experience in the militia, serving as a lieutenant on Colonel David Williamson's expedition and Colonel William Crawford's expedition, both in 1782 ("The Sandusky Expedition," *Pennsylvania Archives, Series 2, Volume 14*, pp. 716, 753); deposition of Hugh Forbes, October 13, 1832, in Andrew Vaneman, Revolutionary War pension application, Pennsylvania, S. 6292.

[49] Lyman Draper interview with William Harrod, Jr., Draper MSS 37J171.

[50] James Marshel to Thomas Mifflin, April 11, 1791, *Pennsylvania Archives, Series 2, Volume 4*, pp. 553-554.

[51] Jacob Crow (c1732-1823), a German immigrant, settled on a 351-acre tract named "Peter," located near the present-day line between Greene County, Pennsylvania, and Marshall County, West Virginia. At the time he settled, the area was part of Virginia, and he is probably the Jacob Crow who served in Captain Daniel Smith's Virginia company during the Revolutionary War (1776). Two of Jacob's sons—Frederick and Martin—also served in the war. Another son, John Crow, was killed by Indians while out hunting on Fishing Creek in 1789. Jacob and his wife Susannah (Secris) had twelve children. Andrew Waychoff, *Local History of Greene County and Southwestern Pennsylvania* (Waynesburg, PA, 1975, from a series of articles published in the *Waynesburg Democrat-Messenger* before 1927), p. 91; James Crow, *Fireside Stories of the Jacob Crow Family* (Parsons, WV, 1979), pp. 123-127; W.F. Horn, *Horn Papers, Early Westward*

Movement on the Monongahela and Upper Ohio, 1765-1795, Volume 3 (Waynesburg, PA, 1945), p. 43; John Gwathmey, *Historical Register of Virginians in the Revolution* (Richmond, VA, 1938), p. 195; Catharine Fedorchak, *Monroe County, Ohio, Genealogical Records, Volume 6*, pp. 80-82.

[52] William Spicer (c1763-) was captured and carried off to Ohio when he was eleven years old and raised by the Indians. He and his sister were taken at the time their parents were killed by a Mingo war party in 1774, about three miles south of Garard's Fort in Dunkard Township (in present-day Greene County, Pennsylvania). Andrew Waychoff, *Local History of Greene County*, pp. 92-97.

[53] The story of the Crow family tragedy has been told in many places. The version included here is from Andrew Waychoff, *Local History of Greene County*, pp. 91-92, 114.

Christina Crow (1783-1853) survived her ordeal with the Indians. She married John McBride and they raised twelve children in Noble County, Ohio. Catharine Fedorchak, *Monroe County, Ohio, Genealogical Records, Volume 6*, pp. 80-81; James Crow, *Fireside Stories of the Jacob Crow Family*, p. 128.

Lindley's Fort was located near present-day Prosperity in Washington County. It was built by Demas Lindley, who came from New Jersey to Morris Township in 1773 with his brothers, Caleb, John and Levi. Demas patented a tract called "Mill Place," where he built his fort and grist mill. The area was later known as "Lindley's Mills." Boyd Crumrine, *History of Washington County*, p. 843; J.H. Beers, *Commemorative Record, Washington County, Pennsylvania* (Chicago, 1893), p. 508.

[54] The distance from place to place along the Ohio River is usually reported in river miles. For later reference, it may be helpful to give the mileage of frequently mentioned locations taken from

topo maps. Starting from mile 0 at Pittsburgh: Wheeling (90 miles); Tomlinson's Fort at Grave Creek (102 miles); Dilles Bottom (102-104 miles); Round Bottom (104-108 miles); Powhatan Point at the mouth of Captina Creek (109½ miles); Baker's Fort at Graveyard Run (110½ miles), Cresap Bottom (110½-113¾ miles); mouth of Fish Creek (113¾ miles).

[55] In 1791 the capital was located in Philadelphia. The new government met in New York City in 1789, then moved to Philadelphia in 1790. The capital did not relocate to the new Federal City—Washington, DC—until 1800.

[56] David Shepherd to Henry Knox, May 6, 1791, Draper MSS 3SS37. The document is in Shepherd's handwriting. Draper managed to obtain most of David Shepherd's papers, accounts books, journals, etc.

[57] Robert Kirkwood (1756-1791), son of a Scottish immigrant, was born on a farm near Newark, Delaware, and educated for the ministry. His education was interrupted by the Revolutionary War. He enlisted in Colonel Hazlet's Delaware regiment in 1776 and served as a captain throughout the war. He participated in the battles of Long Island, Princeton, Trenton, Brandywine, Germantown, Camden, Cowpens, Guilford Courthouse, Ninety-Six, Eutaw Springs and others—each of which he recorded in his journal. After the war he married Sarah England, and they had three children. In 1787 Kirkwood received a grant from Virginia for 2,000 acres in the Seven Ranges, Northwest Territory. He settled on his land in present-day Belmont County, Ohio, in 1790, one of the few residents west of the river at that time. He served as a justice of the peace in the Northwest Territory. Kirkwood enlisted in the U.S. Army in 1791 and joined the ill-fated expedition of General St. Clair. He was killed in action near Fort Recovery in November 1791—"his thirty-third engagement."

The first township in Belmont County was named in honor of Robert Kirkwood. His son Joseph returned to live on the father's land. Robert Kirkwood, *Journal and Order Book of Captain Robert Kirkwood*, Joseph Turner, editor (Port Washington, NY, 1970), pp. 3-6; P. Benson Delany, "Biographical Sketch of Robert Kirkwood," *Graham's Magazine 28* (March 1846), pp. 97-104.

[58] The term "spies" was used in those days to mean "scouts."

[59] Draper MSS 3S148-149.

[60] Draper MSS 2S54-55, 108, 189; Benson Delany, "Biographical Sketch of Robert Kirkwood," p. 102. Accounts of this affair may also be found in Wills de Hass, *History of the Early Settlement and Indian Wars*, pp. 313-315, and Henry Howe, *Historical Collections of Ohio, Volume 1*, p. 314.

[61] Absalom Baird (1758-1805) was the son of John Baird, who came to America with General Braddock's army in 1755. Absalom had just completed his medical studies when the Revolutionary War broke out. He served as a surgeon in the Pennsylvania Line. In 1786 Dr. Baird moved his family to Washington, Pennsylvania. After the war, in 1790, he succeeded James Marshel as county lieutenant and then served as brigade inspector until his death. (In 1793 the office of county lieutenant was abolished and replaced by the brigade inspector.) Boyd Crumrine, *History of Washington County*, pp. 541-542.

[62] Absalom Baird provided written certification of Biggs's and Hedges's conditions, Draper MSS 3SS35. Biggs and Hedges were listed in the census of Revolutionary War pensioners of 1835; Biggs was placed on the pension roll in June 1791 at $108

per annum and Hedges in September 1796 at $60 per annum. Virgil Lewis, *Soldiery of West Virginia*, in Jim Comstock, *West Virginia Heritage Encyclopedia, Volume 9, Supplemental Series* (Richmond, WV, 1974, reprint of 1911 edition), p. 68.

[63] At Samuel Brady's trial, proof was provided that the Delaware were responsible for these attacks. *Pittsburgh Gazette*, May 25, 1793.

[64] Henry Knox to Beverly Randolph, May 31, 1791, *Calendar of Virginia State Papers 5* (1885), p. 319.

[65] David Shepherd to Beverly Randolph, May 9, 1791, *Calendar of Virginia State Papers 5* (1885), p. 301.

[66] From an article written in 1851 by Judge Thomas Scott, Chillicothe, Ohio, and copied by Lyman Draper, Draper MSS 9ZZ84-86.

[67] Donald Jackson, editor, *Diaries of George Washington, Volume 1* (Charlottesville, VA, 1976), p. 298.

[68] Two of John Baker's descendants described the fort in later years. Samuel P. Baker, grandson of John Baker, was born in 1798 and lived near Benwood in Marshall County. In 1866, at the time of his account, Samuel was the oldest native of the county. He is probably the most credible authority on the date of the fort's construction:

> In the year 1784 my father built what was long known as Baker's station, near Cresap's grove. In the same year a family by the name of Parr settled in the Flats, and a short time thereafter Henry Baker married one of his daughters. (from the *Wheeling Intelligencer*, May 1866,

quoted in J.H. Newton, editor, *History of the Panhandle, Being Historical Collections of the Counties of Ohio, Brooke, Marshall and Hancock, West Virginia* (Wheeling, WV, 1879), p. 362)

Arthur O. Baker, great-grandson of John Baker, was born in about 1827 and was the clerk for the circuit court of Marshall County. He wrote to Lyman C. Draper on August 10, 1887, giving his version of the early days at the fort:

> My belief is that Baker's Station was built about 1778, or about that time. Just after that time Captain John Baker, Henry's brother, had a Skirmish at the Big Spring with the Indians, and [the Indians] defeated them, which gave the name of Grave Yard run. They were burried where they fell. Martin Baker and Martin Wetzel were boath there. . . . The Station was just at the head of Cresap's bottom. [Michael Cresap was] the Grand Father of Friend Cox, Esquire, who now lives and owns part of the Michael Cresap estate, but came there long after the Bakers. (Draper MSS 31J103)

In spite of his boast to Draper that he knew more of the family traditions than any of his Uncle Samuel Baker's children, Arthur's date does not square with historical data. It appears that he may have formed his conclusion from a description of Captain John Baker's death that appeared in *History of the Panhandle* (p. 363)—with the wrong date. Baker was killed across the Ohio River from his fort in 1787, not 1778 as stated in *History of the Panhandle.*

[69] Friend Cox to Lyman Draper, November 29, 1886, Draper MSS 14J3. Friend Cox was a grandson of Michael Cresap, Jr.

[70] In 1787 Captain John Baker shot and killed an Indian on the other side of the Ohio River from his fort. Baker and several of

the Wetzel brothers who were with him immediately crossed the river to scalp the Indian, and there Baker was killed. The Wetzels brought his body back and Baker was buried in the little graveyard behind his fort. That same year Martin Wetzel, patriarch of the Wetzel family in Ohio County, was also killed by Indians while paddling his canoe near the mouth of Captina. He too was buried at the fort.

[71] Michael Cresap (1742-1775) was a son of the famous frontiersman and Indian-fighter, Thomas Cresap. Michael achieved some notoriety in his own right, being erroneously charged with the murder of Chief Logan's family in 1774. In 1775, Captain Michael Cresap raised a company of volunteers and marched off to join Washington's army. Michael became ill along the way, died in New York City and was buried in the Trinity Church cemetery.

Cresap made an improvement in the Round Bottom in 1771, the same year George Washington had his tract surveyed. In 1781, his son, Michael, Jr., obtained a settlement certificate for his father's claim and was awarded a patent in 1787. Part of this tract interfered with Washington's claim, however, and Cresap lost most of his land in Round Bottom. Michael, Jr., later settled at Cresap Bottom. J.H. Newton, editor, *History of the Panhandle, Being Historical Collections of the Counties of Ohio, Brooke, Marshall and Hancock, West Virginia* (Wheeling, WV, 1879), pp. 374-376.

[72] Fortescue Cumings, "Sketches of a Tour to the Western Country," in Reuben Thwaites, *Early Western Travels, Volume 4*, p. 117. George Washington did not mention the presence of any settlements on Captina Creek or in Cresap Bottom in 1770. Another traveler, botanist Andre Michaux, wrote in his journal on August 19, 1793, that "there are no settlements between Willing [Wheeling] and Marietta, a small Town situate at the mouth of

the Muskingum river." Michaux must have been referring to the absence of villages rather than settlers. Andre Michaux, "Journal of Andre Michaux," *1793-1796*, in Reuben Thwaites, *Early Western Travels, Volume 3* (Cleveland, 1904), p. 33.

[73] Thaddeus Harris, "Journal of a Tour into the Territory Northwest of the Alleghany Mountains," in Reuben Thwaites, *Early Western Travels, Volume 3*, p. 353.

[74] Fortescue Cumings, "Sketches of a Tour to the Western Country," p. 118.

[75] Harris's description of the terrain, nearly two hundred years ago, is still accurate; he wrote:

> From Fish Creek, on the Virginia shore, the country is flat on the banks of the river; and, on the opposite side, generally broken and rough, without much bottom-land; the mountains and hills mostly rising contiguous to the edge of the river. But, below the islands called "The Three Brothers, " the bottom-lands on the northwest side are extensive and rich.

Thaddeus Harris, "Journal of a Tour into the Territory Northwest of the Alleghany Mountains," p. 350.

[76] Donald Jackson, *Diaries of George Washington, Volume 1*, pp. 298-299.

[77] Both grape vines and Indian artifacts were once plentiful along Captina Creek:

> From the number of flint arrow heads found along Captina valley, we conclude it must have been a favorite hunting ground for the Indians. . . . An Indian village

called "Grape Vine Town," in the Captina valley, consisting of a few huts, or wigwams, was a place visited by white traders from 1764 to 1770. In the fall of the latter year, Gen. Washington, while making his tour down the Ohio, makes mention of it in his journal, and describes it as being eight miles up the stream (Captina) from its mouth. Of course the distance was estimated, and was taken by the meanderings of the stream. . . . After a diligent search, we have arrived at the conclusion that the village was most probably situated on the farm settled and entered by John Bryson, in York township, now [1880] owned by Isaac Ramsey. An unusual number of grape vines were found on this tract by Mr. Bryson when he first settled, and a place or two in the bottom was found to be trampled hard when it was first plowed.

J.A. Caldwell, *History of Belmont and Jefferson Counties, Ohio,* p. 418.

[78] Fort Henry does not merit a mention in the current edition of *The Wheeling Guide* (1997-98), a publication that directs tourists to local "attractions."

[79] Ohio Extension Homemakers, *Belmont County History* (Salem, WV, 1988), p. 107.

[80] Americana Park was established in 1965 and closed in 1991. Riverview Cemetery is on Alternate Route 2 at the northeast end of Round Bottom; McCreary Cemetery is on McCreary Ridge, Route 7, in the Webster District. Naomi Lowe, Moundsville, WV, personal communication.

[81] Lyman Draper to Jeremiah Hollister, March 12, 1862, Draper MSS 7E31; Jeremiah Hollister to Lyman Draper, March 20, 1862, Draper MSS 7E34.

[82] "A Payroll of a Detachment of Washington County Militia in the State of Pennsylvania, under the Command of Sergeant Abner Braddock, in the Service of the United States, by Order of the Lieutenant of Said County," *Pennsylvania Archives, Series 6, Volume 5*, p. 563.

[83] Thomas Ryerson, an early resident of Washington County, was appointed associate judge in 1789 and elected to the General Assembly in 1790. In 1792 Ryerson, Ellis Bane and twenty-three others signed a petition to have Finley Township divided. The new township formed was Richhill, which in 1796 became part of Greene County. Ryerson owned several thousand acres of land in Richhill Township. It was on his 406-acre tract between the North and South forks of Dunkard, named "Vineyard," that Ryerson's Station was built. Ryerson obtained the land from Colonel Henry Enoch, for whom it had been surveyed in 1787. There were two Ryerson's Stations located on the Dunkard fork: a military blockhouse near the forks that was built and used by the militia and a settlers' fort farther up the South fork that had probably been built somewhat earlier by Thomas Ryerson. Andrew Waychoff, *Local History of Greene County*, p. 32; Boyd Crumrine, *History of Washington County*, pp. 249, 471, 775; W.F. Horn, *Horn Papers, Volume 3*, p. 43.

[84] Two Crow daughters were killed by the Indians; a third daughter was seriously wounded and died a few days after the attack. Susannah Crow survived her husband Jacob by some years, thus explaining Harrod's reference to "the widow Crow."

[85] Homer Clark, *Last of the Rangers* (Washington, PA, 1906), p. 8. An historical highway marker at Graysville reads as follows:

> Approximately 100 yards N.E. is former site of Fort Enoch built by Henry Enoch Sr. son of Enoch Enix ca. 1787 for protection against Indians. Pioneer David Gray for whom this village is named, tomahawked a homestead of 2174 A. here in 1768 and became owner of Fort Enoch ca. 1769; enlarged it and renamed it Fort Gray. . . .

Unfortunately, some of the information above—including Henry Enoch being the son of "Enoch Enix"—is not reliable and appears to have been taken from the writings of William Franklin Horn, author of *The Horn Papers*. The first two volumes of this work have been discredited. Arthur Middleton and Douglass Adair, "The Mystery of the Horn Papers," *William and Mary Quarterly, Series 3, Volume 4* (October 1947), pp. 409-445.

Greene County historian Howard Leckey was of the opinion that William Enoch built Fort Enoch sometime after the Revolutionary War. The Enoch family did have a history of militia service at Ryerson's Station and at this Fort Enoch. Howard Leckey, *Tenmile Country and Its Pioneer Families* (Apollo, PA, 1993, reprint of the multivolume 1950 edition), p. 51.

There were two other Fort Enochs in Washington County, both built early in the Revolutionary War or just before. One was at the forks of Tenmile, near Clarksville, and one was in Bethlehem Township, east of North Ten Mile Baptist Church.

[86] Scott Powell, *History of Marshall County [WV] from Forest to Field* (Moundsville, WV, 1925), pp. 80-81; Phyllis Slater, "Warrior Path," *Tri-County Researcher 2* (1978), p. 134. Another ridge trail connects Ryerson's and Moundsville and could have brought the Rangers—or a portion of them—to the river near the mouth of Big Grave Creek.

[87] Lyman Draper to Jeremiah Hollister, March 12, 1862, Draper MSS 7E31.

[88] Martin Baker had four sisters, Catherine and Margaret (twins), Elizabeth and Mary. Catharine Fedorchak, *Monroe County, Ohio, Genealogical Records, Volume 12*, p. 104.

[89] For an informative discussion of this issue, see Elizabeth Perkins, "Border Life, Experience and Perception in the Revolutionary Ohio Valley," Ph.D. dissertation, Northwestern University (Chicago, 1992), pp. 228-249.

[90] The whereabouts of Henry and William Enoch at this time is uncertain. John Shoptaw, who joined a Ranger company as a volunteer, stated that

> The officers of said Company was Captain Henry Enochs, Lieutenant William Enochs and Ensign Abraham Enochs.

These men were brothers, all sons of Colonel Henry Enoch, Sr., who had served on the frontiers throughout the Revolutionary War. William Harrod reported that William Enoch led the company from Ryerson's Station in pursuit of the Indians. Duncan McArthur was a volunteer in the "company commanded by Captain William Enoch," but McArthur clearly indicates that Abraham Enoch led the party on the second day—an unlikely event if the higher ranking William was present.

With the number of Enoch men involved, it may be that some of the names were misremembered in later years. Certainly, their ranks were. Although referred to as a lieutenant in some accounts and a captain in others, Abraham Enoch was an ensign, as stated in Colonel David Shepherd's dispatch of May 6. Shepherd gives Joseph Biggs's rank as ensign, which is confirmed by an Ohio County militia pay abstract (Draper MSS 3SS77). Many accounts incorrectly refer to Joseph as "Captain Biggs." Rank, it seems, was loosely recalled in later years.

There seems to be a consensus that Abraham was present and led the party, as reported by McArthur, McKiernan, Tomlinson, Baker and Hollister. It is conceivable that either Henry or William Enoch, or both, were along on the mission and that their presence went unreported, but this is unlikely. One account, Harrod's, could be taken as indirect evidence for William Enoch's participation. Harrod's account states that "Captain Enochs killed one Indian." Since Harrod had already referred to "Captain William Enochs," it seems that he is saying William was the one who killed an Indian. Draper, who transcribed Harrod's statement, may have misunderstood which Enoch was being spoken of. That this was the case is suggested by Harrod's statement that Abraham was "in the advance" and by all the other accounts, which state that Abraham killed an Indian. McArthur's biography emphatically states that after "Lieutenant Enoch" was killed, "no officer was left to command."

The most likely alternative is that William and Henry were elsewhere that day. One of the brothers—Henry, who is only mentioned by Shoptaw—may have stayed at Ryerson's or may have been out "scouring" somewhere else at the time. William Enoch, who probably did set off in pursuit, may have split his company while searching for the Indians. He may have taken a northern route with part of the company, heading toward Tomlinson's, and sent part of his company to Baker's Fort via the old Warrior Trail that paralleled Fish Creek. Whatever the explanation, the weight of evidence suggests that Henry and William Enoch were not in the party that engaged the Indians on Captina on the second day. And since they were not involved in the action, their whereabouts that day went unreported.

There is another inconsistency in the accounts to explain. The reporters seem to agree that all able-bodied men volunteered and that Abraham Enoch's force consisted of fifteen to twenty men. Yet Martin Baker said that there were about fifty men at the fort that day. This would make sense if there were two parties that went out from Baker's, with fifteen to twenty men each, leaving ten or so behind, including old men and the scout, John Shoptaw, who may have been wounded. This second party could account for William Enoch on the second day. It is possible to envision tactics that would involve two groups of Rangers going out from Baker's Fort. The weakness of this idea, however, is the fact that none of the reports makes any mention of a "second party."

[91] From the description, this point would be on the present site of the Clair Mar Golf Course on Route 148.

[92] One secondary account places the battle at the mouth of Cat's Run, which enters Captina Creek from the northwest, about two miles from the Ohio River. No source was given and none of the other accounts support this location. Scott Powell, *History of Marshall County*, pp. 73-74.

[93] The men may have been looking for the body of John Daniels, whom they presumed had been killed along with Adam Miller. They may not have learned otherwise until Daniels returned from captivity.

[94] From the journal of Judge Lewis Summers, copied in J.H. Brantner, *Historical Collections of Moundsville, West Virginia* (Moundsville, WV, 1947), p. 179.

[95] Richard Butler to David Shepherd, June 11, 1791, Draper MSS 3SS43.

[96] Boyd Crumrine, *History of Washington County*, pp. 224-225; Virgil Lewis, *Soldiery of West Virginia*, p. 120. In January

1790, President Washington presented to Congress Henry Knox's plan for revamping the militia system. The customary militia would be formed of men aged twenty-one through forty-five. Eighteen, nineteen and twenty year olds would be placed in a separate training class called the "advanced corps." Men from forty-six to sixty would be placed in the "reserve corps," subject to be called out only in the event of an invasion. U.S. Congress, *American State Papers, Military Affairs, Volume 1*, pp. 6-13.

[97] Fred Berg, *Encyclopedia of Continental Army Units* (Harrisburg, PA, 1972), p. 104.

[98] Abraham Enoch was probably one of the latter, as there is no record of his previous service as an officer.

[99] Catharine Fedorchak, *Monroe County, Ohio, Genealogical Records, Volume 6*, pp. 82-86; J.H. Newton, *History of the Panhandle*, pp. 361-363.

[100] Virgin's Blockhouse was a few miles southwest of Washington near the head of Chartiers Creek; Atkinson's Fort was near the head of the Little Tenmile Creek, only a few miles from Virgin's. Both were in Franklin Township. The Atkinsons, Virgins and Craycrafts were all neighbors. Boyd Crumrine, *History of Washington County,* pp. 797, 799.

[101] Daniel Bean, Revolutionary War pension application, Pennsylvania, W. 8124.

[102] J.A. Caldwell, *History of Belmont and Jefferson Counties, Ohio,* p. 414. "Daniel and Jesse Bean" along with John Dailey and Joseph Baker are identified as early settlers of Monroe

County. H.H. Hardesty, *History of Monroe County, Ohio* (Chicago, 1882), p. 213.

[103] Additional evidence that this is the same Daniel Bain that fought at Captina is provided by Hollister; after describing Bain's participation in the battle, he wrote that later on "Daniel Bean removed to Muskingum County Ohio where he obtained a pension under the act June 7th 1832." Jeremiah Hollister to Lyman Draper, May 20, 1862, Draper MSS 7E42.

[104] James Gaylord, *Historical Reminiscences of Morgan County, Ohio* (n.p., 1984, reprinted from *The Weekly Herald*, McConnelsville, Ohio, 1932), p. 41.

[105] Lee Bain, *Daniel Bain, Frontiersman, 1764-1840, A Documentary Account of His Life and Line* (Rolla, MO, 1988); Daniel Bean, Revolutionary War pension application, Pennsylvania, W. 8124, BLW 67698-160-55; Draper MSS 3SS189-190.

[106] Charles Craycraft (c1766-1832) married John Bain's sister, Mary. Charles served in the Revolutionary War—later receiving a pension—and throughout the Indian Wars. During the Revolution he volunteered at age fourteen while living in Hampshire County, Virginia. He served with his brother, Joseph, who entered service as a substitute for their father, Samuel Craycraft. Charles moved to Ohio in 1803 and then to Greenup County, Kentucky, where he married Elizabeth Dillon in 1828. Charles Craycraft, Revolutionary War pension application, Virginia, W. 10228

[107] Lyman Draper interview with Isaac Bane, Jr., no date, Draper MSS 2S9-11.

Notes

[108] Elisha Bain to Lyman Draper, undated, Draper MSS 2E28.

[109] In the census of military pensioners taken in 1840, a John Bain, age seventy-two (thus born c1768), is on the list for Morgan County, Ohio. There were two John Bains in Morgan County, however, and it is not clear which one received the pension. The John Bain of this sketch could have been no more than fifteen years old in 1783, the last year of the war. While that sounds very young to have served in the war, it was not unheard of. As mentioned above, Charles Craycraft, John's brother-in-law, enlisted at age fourteen. Charles Craycraft, Revolutionary War pension application, Virginia, W. 10228

Efforts to locate John Bain's Revolutionary War pension papers have been unsuccessful; only the supporting depositions of John Dailey and John Yoho are known at this time, and they are with the Draper manuscripts, not in the National Archives.

[110] Hollister knew this to be the John Bain who was at Captina and wrote of him as follows:

> I have learned further that Jack Bean when he left Captina settled on the big Buffalow fork of Wills Creek at a place now caled Cumberland. I believe in Morgan County Ohio [actually was in Guernsey County].

Jeremiah Hollister to Lyman Draper, May 20, 1862, Draper MSS 7E42.

[111] Lee Bain, *Daniel Bain, Frontiersman, 1764-1840, A Documentary Account of His Life and Line; Pennsylvania Archives,* Series 6, Volume 2, pp. 101, 121; Series 6, Volume 5, pp. 595-597; Draper MSS 2E28; 2S9-11; 4SS103; Howard Leckey, *Tenmile Country and Its Pioneer Families,* p. 143; J.A. Caldwell, *History of Belmont and Jefferson Counties, Ohio,* p. 426.

[112] Frank Bane, *John Bane of Short Creek, West Virginia and His Descendants* (Fairview, WV, 1956).

[113] Jeremiah Hollister to Lyman Draper, November 4, 1861, Draper MSS 7E39.

[114] Brant and Fuller, *History of the Upper Ohio Valley, Volume 1* (Madison, WI, 1890), pp. 185-186.

[115] Brant and Fuller, *History of the Upper Ohio Valley, Volume 1*, pp. 184, 186; Grace Tracey and John Dern, *Pioneers of Old Monocacy* (Baltimore, 1987), pp. 309-311; Ross Johnston, *West Virginians in the American Revolution* (Baltimore, 1977, reprinted in 1995), pp. 18-19; Catharine Fedorchak, *Monroe County, Ohio, Genealogical Records, Volume 5*, p. 17; Howard Leckey, *Tenmile Country and Its Pioneer Families*, p. 258; J.H. Brantner, *Historical Collections of Moundsville, West Virginia*, p. 40; Joseph Biggs, Revolutionary War pension application, Virginia, R. 831; U.S. Secretary of War, *Transcript of the Pension List of the United States* (Baltimore, 1953, reprint of the 1813 document);

[116] J.A. Caldwell, *History of Belmont and Jefferson Counties, Ohio*, p. 174.

[117] J.A. Caldwell, *History of Belmont and Jefferson Counties, Ohio*, pp. 164, 173-174, 179, 249; Belmont County Common Pleas Court, June 1824, *James R. Boggs et al. vs Margaret Boggs et al.*, in Ruth Bowers and Anita Short, *Gateway to the West, Volume 1* (Baltimore, 1989), p. 113.

[118] Catharine Fedorchak, *Monroe County, Ohio, Genealogical Records, Volume 3*, p.26, and *Volume 9*, p. 92; Ohio County

militia pay roll for 1791, Draper MSS 3SS75-83; pay roll for Captain Seals's company, *Pennsylvania Archives, Series 6, Volume 5*, pp. 619, 633; H.H. Hardesty, *History of Monroe County, Ohio* (Chicago, 1892), p. 213.

[119] Captain James O'Hara's muster roll of Independent company of Regulars stationed at Fort Pitt, October 1, 1777, Draper MSS 3NN6-7; Lyman Draper interview with Phebe Miranda, Draper MSS 2S256-260; John Gwathmey, *Historical Register of Virginians in the Revolution*, p. 256.

[120] Helen Vogt, *Westward of ye Laurall Hills* (Brownsville, PA, 1976), p. 157. This information was taken from the 1798 Direct Tax.

[121] Helen Vogt, *Westward of ye Laurall Hills*, pp. 152-157; Shirley Mikesell, *Early Settlers of Montgomery County, Ohio, Genealogical Abstracts from Common Pleas Court Records, Civil and Probate* (Bowie, MD, 1992). pp. 40, 44, 54, 106, 146, 176-177, 186, 212, 239; W.H. Beers, *History of Montgomery County, Ohio* (Chicago, 1882), part 3, pp. 83-84.

[122] *Pennsylvania Archives, Series 6, Volume 2*, pp. 14, 237, 249, 255; Executive minutes, January 19 and February 23, 1792, *Pennsylvania Archives, Series 9, Volume 1*, pp. 317, 329; Return of the officers elected in the 2nd Regiment of the 2nd Brigade of Washington County, Thomas Wolverton, Lieutenant Colonel commanding, *Pennsylvania Archives, Series 9, Volume 1*, pp. 645-646.

[123] *Western Telegraphe and Washington Advertiser* (Washington, Pennsylvania), April 1797, quoted in Helen Vogt, *Westward of ye Laurall Hills*, pp. 181-182.

[124] Helen Vogt, et al., *Genealogy and Biographical Sketches of Descendants of Abraham Tegarden* (Berkeley, CA, 1988, revision of the 1967 edition), pp. 69-73; Helen Vogt, *Westward of ye Laurall Hills*, pp. 151-156; Donald Black, *History of Wood County, West Virginia, Volume 1* (Marietta, OH, 1975), pp. 4-4, 7-2, 7-11; Melba Zinn, *Monongalia County (West) Virginia, Records of the District, Superior and County Courts, Volumes 2 and 3* (Bowie, MD, 1990); Barbara Wolfe, *Lost Soldiers, An Index to the Compiled Service Records of Volunteer Soldiers, 1784-1811* (Indianapolis, IN, 1985); W.H. Beers, *History of Clark County, Ohio* (Chicago, 1881), pp. 291, 612, 686, 690; *Pennsylvania Archives, Series 6, Volume 2*, pp. 254-255; *Series 9, Volume 1*, p. 645; *Series 9, Volume 2*, p. 1154.

[125] James Finley, *Autobiography of Reverend James Finley* (Cincinnati, 1853), p. 122.

[126] John McDonald, *Biographical Sketches of General Nathaniel Massie, General Duncan McArthur, Captain William Wells and General Simon Kenton* (Cincinnati, 1838), pp. 71-181; Western Biographical Publishing Company, *Biographical Cyclopedia and Portrait Gallery of Ohio, Volume 1* (Cincinnati, 1894), p. 101; Williams Brothers Publishers, *History of Ross and Highland Counties* (Cleveland, 1880) p. 221-222; Ohio Historical Society, *Governors of Ohio* (Columbus, 1969); C.H. Cramer, "Duncan McArthur, First Phase, 1772-1812," *Ohio Archaeological and Historical Quarterly 45* (1936), pp. 27-33; Clara Duer, *Pittsburgh Gazette Abstracts, 1786-1797*, pp. 25, 29; Boyd Crumrine, *History of Washington County*, p. 982; W.F. Horn, *Horn Papers, Volume 3*, p. 64; *Pennsylvania Archives, Series 6, Volume 5*, p. 574; *Series 9, Volume 1*, p. 470.

[127] Joseph Doddridge, *Notes on the Settlement and Indian Wars,* pp. 274-278; Wills de Hass, *History of the Early Settlement and Indian Wars,* pp. 338-344; Samuel Kercheval, *History of the Valley of Virginia* (Woodstock, VA, 1850, second edition), p. 162; J.H. Newton, *History of the Panhandle,* pp. 158-159; Draper MSS 3SS22, 77, 79, 151-152, 179-180; Lyman Draper interview with Samuel Hedges, Draper 19S215, 217, 220; Raymond Bell, "McColloch of Ohio County, West Virginia," *The Keyhole, Quarterly of the Genealogical Society of Southwestern Pennsylvania 13* (1985), p. 100.

[128] Boyd Crumrine, *History of Washington County,* pp. 911-912; Boyd Crumrine, "Civil and Legal History," in *Centennial Celebration of the Organization of Washington County, Pennsylvania, Proceedings and Addresses* (Washington, PA, 1881), p. 32; *Pennsylvania Archives, Series 6, Volume 2,* pp. 106-107; Draper MSS 13CC218.

[129] Elizabeth Hack, *History of the Jacob Miller Family of Donegal Township, Washington County, Pennsylvania* (Indianapolis, 1955), pp. 5-22; Boyd Crumrine, *History of Washington County,* p. 112; *Pennsylvania Archives, Series 6, Volume 4,* pp. 323.

[130] Washington County Orphan Court Records, Book A-1, p. 35; Elizabeth Hack, *History of the Jacob Miller Family,* pp. 16, 21-22; Raymond Bell, "More on the Jacob Miller, Sr., Family of Donegal Township, Washington County, Pennsylvania," *The Keyhole, Quarterly of the Genealogical Society of Southwestern Pennsylvania 6* (1978), p. 121, and "Indian Attacks on Five Neighboring Families," *ibid., 17* (1989), p. 10; John Shoptaw, Revolutionary War pension application, Pennsylvania, O.W. Rej. 21684.

[131] Laura Shoptaugh, *Some Descendants of Jonas Halsted (1610-1682) and Some Allied Families* (Oakland, CA, 1954), pp. 106-127; John Shoptaw, Revolutionary War pension application, Pennsylvania, O.W. Rej. 21684.

[132] Catharine Fedorchak, *Monroe County, Ohio, Genealogical Records*, Volume 12, pp. 93-111; J.H. Newton, *History of the Panhandle*, pp. 361-362.

[133] *Pennsylvania Archives*, Series 6, Volume 2, p. 229; Series 6, Volume 5, pp. 618-620, 634; Boyd Crumrine, *History of Washington County*, pp. 700-701.

[134] W.F. Horn, *Horn Papers*, Volume 3, p. 77; Revolutionary War pension applications: James Dobbin, Pennsylvania, S. 22732, and John Dobbins, Pennsylvania, W. 3784; *Pennsylvania Archives*, Series 9, Volume 2, p. 1397.

A James Dobbings applied for a pension for service in the Pennsylvania Line, but he went to Kentucky after the war. James Dobbings, Revolutionary War pension application, Maryland and Pennsylvania, R. 2979.

[135] Draper MSS 26CC45; 3SS191-193; *Pennsylvania Archives*, Series 6, Volume 2, pp. 100-101; Series 3, Volume 22, p. 741; Henry Howe, *Historical Collections of Ohio*, Volume 2, pp. 608-610; Virgil White, *Genealogical Abstracts of Revolutionary War Pension Files, Volume 1* (Waynesboro, TN, 1990), pp. 1017-1018.

[136] Boyd Crumrine, *History of Washington County*, p. 934; Jerry Clouse, *Whiskey Rebellion, Southwestern Pennsylvania's Frontier People Test the American Constitution* (Harrisburg, 1994), p. 71; *Pennsylvania Archives*, Series 6, Volume 2, pp. 17, 172,

174, 194, 198, 204, 212; Virgil White, *Genealogical Abstracts of Revolutionary War Pension Files, Volume 2*, pp. 1666-1667, 1751; H.H. Hardesty, *History of Monroe County, Ohio*, p. 23.

[137] Revolutionary War pension applications: Joseph Line, Virginia, R. 6359, and John Line, Virginia, S. 18491; *Pennsylvania Archives, Series 3, Volume 22*, p. 747; Howard Leckey, *Tenmile Country and Its Pioneer Families*, pp. 34, 130-131; Barbara Adams and Gene Mozley, *Memorial Records of Shelby County, Ohio* (Baltimore, 1977), p. 381; Daughters of the American Revolution, *Official Roster of the Soldiers of the American Revolution Buried in the State of Ohio, Volume 1* (Columbus, 1929), p. 228.

[138] *Pennsylvania Archives, Series 3, Volume 22*, pp. 701-782. There are several Cowens/Cowans listed in the 1790 Washington County census, including an Isaac Cowen with a household of four males and three females. John, Hugh and William Cowan are found on the Washington County muster roll for Captain Andrew Swearingham (Swearingen) in May 1782, along with George McCulloch, Sr. and Jr. In September 1782 Alexander, John, Hugh and William Cowan are on a return of Captain Charles Bilderback, along with George McCullough, Sr. and Jr., and Robert Downing. Most of the Cowen/Cowan family are found in Smith Township. Since their names are consistently spelled without the "Mc," this family would appear to be distinct from the McCowans. *Pennsylvania Archives, Series 6, Volume 2*, pp. 106-107, 113-114, 122-123; *Series 3, Volume 22*, pp. 773-776.

[139] Jeremiah Hollister to Lyman Draper, May 20, 1862, Draper MSS 7E40. John's brother, David, was listed as a resident of Seneca Township, Monroe County, Ohio, in the 1820 census. Margaret Sutherland (1763-1842), "consort of David," is buried in the cemetery at Southerland Methodist Church near Stafford in

Franklin Township. Catharine Fedorchak, *Monroe County, Ohio, Genealogical Records, Volume 3*, pp. 76-77.

[140] John Sutherland, Revolutionary War pension application, Maryland, S. 6173; Boyd Crumrine, *History of Washington County*, p. 980; J.H. Beers, *Commemorative Record, Washington County, Pennsylvania* (Chicago, 1893), p. 758; Alfred Creigh, *History of Washington, Pennsylvania* (Harrisburg, PA, 1871).

[141] Henry Howe, *Historical Collections of Ohio, Volume 2*, pp. 306-307. The date is from a letter describing the incident, probably by David Shepherd; the letter, written just after the massacre, is dated July 22, 1792. Draper MSS 3SS129-130.

The Dille brothers built their fort opposite the mouth of Grave Creek:

> In 1793, John and Samuel Dille settled on land since known as Dille's Bottom. In the same year they built a fort known as Dille's fort for protection of settlers. The following year old man Tate was killed. Brant and Fuller, *History of the Upper Ohio Valley, Volume 2*, p. 454.

Since Tate was killed in 1792, the fort was probably built the year before.

[142] Deposition of Daniel Hamilton, October 5, 1832, in Andrew Vaneman, Revolutionary War pension application, Pennsylvania, S. 6292. Hamilton was a resident of Fallowfield Township and a participant in the Whiskey Rebellion, along with his more prominent cousin, Colonel John Hamilton. Daniel was accused of assaulting a revenue collector in 1791. Leland Baldwin, *Whiskey Rebels, The Story of a Frontier Uprising* (Pittsburgh, 1939).

Notes

[143] Boyd Crumrine, *History of Washington County*, pp. 873, 951; Boyd Crumrine, "Civil and Legal History," p. 43; *Pennsylvania Archives, Series 6, Volume 2*, pp. 97, 99, 108, 109, 112, 119; W.F. Horn, *Horn Papers, Volume 3*, pp. 78, 80; Andrew Vaneman, Revolutionary War pension application, Pennsylvania, S. 6292.

[144] Samuel Davis was born in one of the New England states, came down the Ohio River in 1788 or 1789, served at Fort Massie on the Ohio and for a while on the Mississippi, and then settled near Washington in Mason County, Kentucky. There he was one of four scouts for the county militia—the others were Duncan McArthur, Nathaniel Beasly and Samuel McDowell. Davis later settled on the Scioto River in Ohio, where he worked as a gunsmith. He was still alive at the time McDonald wrote the article about him. John McDonald, "A Sketch of the Life and Character of Samuel Davis," *Western Christian Advocate*, November 2, 1835, a copy of which appears in Draper MSS 26CC45-48.

[145] John McDonald, *Biographical Sketches*, pp. 79-80; John McDonald, "A Sketch of the Life and Character of Samuel Davis," Draper MSS 26CC45-48.

[146] G.L. Cranmer, "Colonel David Shepherd," *West Virginia Historical Magazine Quarterly 2* (April 1902), pp. 31-35; Harriett Foster, "Chronological Sketch of Colonel David Shepherd," *West Virginia Historical Magazine Quarterly 3* (January 1903), pp. 67-78.

[147] A transcript also appears in the *Calendar of Virginia State Papers*, albeit with some copy errors and omissions. David Shep-

herd to Henry Knox, May 6, 1791, *Calendar of Virginia State Papers 5* (1885), p. 300.

[148] The issues of the *Gazette* between May 1790 and January 1793 are no longer extant. Clara Duer, *Pittsburgh Gazette Abstracts, 1786-1797*, p. 77.

[149] Located near the head of the North fork of Tenmile Creek in Franklin Township, Washington County. George, John and Thomas Atkinson owned adjoining tracts of land in the area. Boyd Crumrine, *History of Washington County*, p. 799.

[150] Charles Craycraft (c1748-1824) lived near the Atkinsons in Franklin Township. Charles settled early in Washington County and served in the militia throughout the Revolutionary War. He was captured by the Indians while serving in George Rogers Clark's western expedition in 1781. Upon his return, he purchased a tract on Tenmile Creek from William Atkinson and married George Atkinson's daughter, Ellen. Boyd Crumrine, *History of Washington County*, p.776; J.H. Newton, *History of the Panhandle*, p. 298. He may have been an uncle of the Charles Craycraft who was a brother-in-law of John and Daniel Bain.

[151] *Pennsylvania Archives, Series 2, Volume 14;* p. 716, *Series 3, Volume 22*, p. 770.

[152] Thomas Nichols was a resident of Franklin Township, Washington County, where he received a grant for a tract of land called "Crystal." Boyd Crumrine, *History of Washington County*, p. 799.

[153] William Brothers Publishers, *History of Ross and Highland Counties, Ohio*, pp. 221-222.

Notes

[154] John McDonald, *Biographical Sketches*, p. A2.

[155] *Pennsylvania Archives, Series 6, Volume 5*, p. 574; *Series 9, Volume 1, Part 2*, pp. 469-470.

[156] Draper MSS 6ZZ12-13.

[157] George S. McKiernan, letter to editor, *American Pioneer 2* (1843), p. 176.

[158] Joseph Tomlinson's will, Ohio County Will Book 2, p. 262; J.H. Newton, *History of the Panhandle*, pp. 366-376; Brant and Fuller, *History of the Upper Ohio Valley, Volume 1*, pp. 741-742; J.H. Brantner, *Historical Collections of Moundsville, West Virginia*, p. 16.

[159] A.B. Tomlinson, letter to the editor, *American Pioneer 1* (1843), p. 357.

[160] This exploration produced a stone inscribed with crude writing or hieroglyphics. The stone's authenticity became the subject of an intense archaeological debate that, although diminished, continues today. Terry Barnhart, "Curious Antiquity? The Grave Creek Controversy Revisited," *West Virginia History 46* (1985-86), pp. 103-124.

[161] Howard Leckey, *Tenmile Country and Its Pioneer Families*, pp. 240-255; *Pennsylvania Archives, Series 6, Volume 5*, pp. 563, 613.

[162] Catharine Fedorchak, *Monroe County, Ohio, Genealogical Records, Volume 8*, pp. 96-99.

[163] Martin Baker's account has been "lifted" from Howe's book and republished many times, often without credit to Howe. See for example, Scott Powell, *History of Marshall County*, pp. 73-74; J.H. Newton, *History of the Panhandle*, p. 165; J.A. Caldwell, *History of Belmont and Jefferson Counties, Ohio*, p.165; A.T. McKelvey, *Centennial History of Belmont County, Ohio, and Representative Citizens* (Chicago, 1903), pp. 307-308; H.H. Hardesty, *History of Monroe County, Ohio*, p. 205.

[164] Vito Brenni, *West Virginia Authors, A Biobibliography* (Morgantown, WV, 1957), p. 18; A.N. Marquis Company, *Who Was Who in America, Volume 1, 1897-1942* (Chicago, 1943), pp. 310-311.

[165] J.H. Newton, *History of the Panhandle*, pp. 366-371.

[166] A.J. Baughman, *Centennial Biographical History of Richland County, Ohio* (Chicago, 1901), pp. 105-114; Allen Johnson and Dumas Malone, *Dictionary of American Biography, Volume 11* (New York, 1932), pp. 49-50.

[167] Roeliff Brinkerhoff, *A Pioneer History of Richland County, Ohio*, Mary Jane Henney, editor (Mansfield, Ohio, 1993, reprinted from the *Mansfield Herald*, 1855-1859), p. 1.

[168] A.A. Graham, *History of Richland County, Ohio, Its Past and Present* (Mansfield, OH, 1880).

[169] *Spirit of Democracy* (Woodsfield, Ohio), 19 November 1867; H.H. Hardesty, *History of Monroe County, Ohio*, p. 214.

[170] According to McDonald's version, McArthur got tangled up in a tree root, tripped and fell to the ground just as an Indian's shot went overhead. John McDonald, *Biographical Sketches*, p. 87. Another version of the "grapevine incident" is attributed to a "General Weir," who reported he had it from the lips of McArthur himself, and gave the year as 1795—well after Captina. J.A. Caldwell, *History of Belmont and Jefferson Counties, Ohio*, p. 165.

[171] Lyman Draper interview with Samuel Hedges, Draper MSS 19S198-224; Grace Tracey and John Dern, *Pioneers of Old Monocacy*, pp. 106-113.

[172] "An account of monies received for Ohio County Militia agreeably to the pay rolls for services in 1791, by James Marshel Attesting for Colonel David Shepherd," Draper MSS 3SS75-83.

[173] *Pennsylvania Archives, Series 6, Volume 5*, pp. 563-567. There are numerous Washington County rosters containing hundreds of names for the years 1792 to 1795. *Ibid.*, pp. 568-643.

Index

ALLENDER, William 144
ALLWINE, Lawrence 79
ANCRIM, John 129
ANDREWS, James 144
ARMSTRONG, Hugh 144
ASHLIN, Lee 13
ATEN, Curnelis 146
ATHSON, James 144
ATKINSON, 173 Ellen 184 George 184 John 184 Michel 109 Mitchel 110 Thomas 184
AVECOST, Joseph 89
BAIN, 79 Elisha 81 Alva 82 Andrew 79 Ann 82 Bryson 79 Daniel 26 49-50 55 58-59 69 78 80-82 109 114-115 138 142 174 Daniel Jr 79 Delilia 79 Dorcas 82 Elisha 79 82 Elizabeth 79 Hannah 82 Jack 80 82 Jane 82 Jesse 80 John 26 49-50 54-55 58 67 69-70 78-83 108 113-115 138-139 174-175 John Sr 80 Keziah 79 Lorinda 82 Mary 174 Sarah 79 82 Susannah 79 Vincent 79 Zachariah 82
BAIRD, Absalom 30 83 113 162 John 162
BAKER, 28 51 124 126 135 165 171 Arthur 164 Catherine 77-78 94 170 Elisabeth 141 Elizabeth 77-78 170 George 77 141 Henry 58 77-78 141 163-164 Honesley 109 Isaac 78 95 141 Jacob 141 John 20 26-27 38-39 46 58 63-64 67-69 94 123 127 129 131-134 140-143 163-164 John Jr 77-78 John Sr 77 Joseph 58 108 173 Margaret 77-78 94 170 Martin 49-50 53-55 57 63-64 69 77-78 110 129-130 138-139 141-142 164 170-171 186 Mary 78 141 170 Raymond 46 Ross 46 Samuel 163-164 Sarah 129
BALTZELL, Mary 98
BANE, 79 Daniel 78 114-115 Ellis 81 168 Isaac 81 Jesse 81 John 82 108-109 113-115 Joseph Jr 81 Nathan 81

BARBER, Henry 144
BARKER, Eliza 151 Joseph 151
BARR, David 144 Thomas 152
BARRETT, John 30 144
BARTHOLEMEN, John 146
BEAN, 79 135 Dan 80 Daniel 79 109-110 114-115 117 124 140-141 143 173-174 Jack 67 132 138-141 175 Jesse 173 John 80 126 134 140
BEASLY, Nathaniel 183
BEEN, 79 John 80-81
BELL, 129 Benjamin 89 Philip 144
BERDEEN, Nathan 144
BIDDLE, 42
BIGGS, 29-30 162 Allen 83 Benjamin Jr 82 Benjamin Sr 83 Ens 28 51 105 Gen 83 Joe 83 John 82 Joseph 28 70 82-84 113-114 144 152 154 170-171 Mary 84 Mrs 84 Thomas 82 William 82 Zaccheus 82
BIGS, Joseph 107
BILDERBACK, Charles 181
BILDERBECK, Joseph 144
BLACKBURNS, James 87
BLAKENEY, Capt 116 Gabriel 78
BLAKNEY, 116
BLENNERHASSETT, Harmon 151
BOGGS, 30 Alexander 26 58 84-85 136-137 Alice 85 Elizabeth 85 Ezekiel 49-50 84-85 136-137 Francis 85 Hannah 84-85 James 9 85 155 Jane 84-85 136 Lucinda 85 Margaret 85 Reuben 85 William 84-85
BONNET, 83
BONNETT, 22
BOONE, 73 Daniel 58
BOWMAN, Diana 107
BRADDOCK, Abner 128 146 Gen 162
BRADY, 73 154 156 Drusilla 153 Samuel 10 153 155 163
BRINKERHOFF, Roeliff 136-137
BROCK, 109 Capt 85 108 114 Joseph 70 82

Index

BRODHEAD, Gen 80
BROWN, Robert 144
BRUNER, Michael 144
BRYSON, John 167
BUTLER, Richard 70
CAIN, Abel 144
CALDWELL, Samuel 144
CAMP, John 151
CARSON, Robert 144
CHAMBERLAN, Stout 146
CHOAT, Francis 151 Isaac 151
CHOATE, Old Man 80
CHRISTOPHER, Muller 92
CITS, Mary 94-95
CLAFFIN, John 146
CLARK, George Rogers 98 184 Joseph 151
COCHAS, George 144
COLLINS, Hannah 82
CONNER, James 144 John 144
COPUS, James 146
COUCH, James 151
COVALT, Abraham 7
COWAN, Alexander 181 Hugh 181 John 181 William 181
COWEN, Isaac 181
COWHERN, Joseph 146 William 146
COX, Friend 34 38 164
COYLE, William 144
CRACRAFT, Maj 78
CRAWFORD, 82 111 116 Col 78 109 William 38 98 128 159
CRAYCRAFT, 173 Charles 78 80 82 95 110 116 174-175 184 Elizabeth 174 Ellen 184 Joseph 174 Mary 174 Samuel 174
CRESAP, Michael 34 40 164-165 Michael Jr 40 165 Thomas 165
CRESSOP, Michael 42 Mr 40 Mrs 40
CROFFORD, 116
CROGHAN, James 144

CROW, 22 51-53 74 128 Betsy 22 25 Catherine 22 Christina 22 160 Elizabeth 22 Frederick 159 Jacob 22 25 159 168 John 159 Katie 22 25 Martin 159 Michael 25 Susan 22 Susannah 159 168 Susie 25 Tena 22 25 106 Widow 129
CRUMRINE, 95 Boyd 158
CUMINGS, 42 Fortescue 40
CUMMINS, James 128
DAILEY, James 85 John 50 58 69-70 78 84-86 95 108-109 113 144 173 175 Mary 84 Nancy 86
DAILY, John 49 139
DALEY, John 109-110
DANIEL, John 53
DANIELS, 56 111 John 26 28 54-55 66 95 110 112 130 138-141 172
DANILLS, John 95
DARNALD, Cornelius 144 Henry 144 Thomas 144
DARRAH, Joseph 146 Robert 146
DAVIS, David 144 Jesse 144 Jessie 146 Samuel 101-102 120 183
DAWSON, None 146
DEHASS, 54 63-65 68 Dr 45 Wills 49-50 132-133
DELONG, Solomon 144
DEMAS, Jacob 144
DEMENT, William 144
DENMAN, Matthias 4
DICKINSON, Mr 69
DILLE, John 182 Samuel 182
DILLON, Elizabeth 174
DOBBINS, 27 58 96 124 135 Elizabeth 96 James 96 John 96 Lennard 96
DONALD, Henry 95 John 95
DONNELL, Henry 95 John 95 Rebecca 95
DOWNEY, 97 John 97 Patrick 97 Samuel 97 Thomas 97
DOWNING, 27 58 75 96 127 James 96 James Sr 96 John 96 Robert 181 Timothy 96
DRAKE, Peter 94 112

DRAPER, 99 129 139 143 161 171 Lyman 34 49 51 56 59 62 95 105 120 128 138 142 164
DUNCAN, John 144
EATEN, James 146
EDGENTON, George 144 Isaac 144 John 144
ELSON, Susannah 79
ENGLAND, Sarah 161
ENIX, Capt 81 Enoch 169 Lt 57 107
ENNICKS, Abm 86
ENNIX, Abram 86
ENOCH, 28 60 81-82 128 142 Abraham 26-27 58 67 74-75 86 106 111 159 171 173 Abram 131 Capt 78 115-116 Elizabeth 87 Enoch 95 Enoch Jr 95 Henry 21 54 Henry 86 Henry 88 95 111 128-129 168 170-171 Henry Iii 87 Henry Jr 86-87 89 95 110 158 Henry Sr 86-87 169-170 Isaac 87-89 Lt 59 63 87 119-120 171 Mary 88 Widow 87 William 26 52-53 68 86-89 111 118 128 159 169-172
ENOCHS, 69 123-124 135 Abraham 112 122 129 134 139-140 170 Abram 138 Capt 126-127 143 171 Henry 112 170 William 52 112 129 170
ENOCK, Enock Jr 146
ENOX, Ens 28 51 105
ERELWINE, John 144
EVANS, Rebecca 95
FAIRLEY, Andrew 87 97
FARNSWORTH, Sarah 129
FARWELL, Jonathan 151
FERREL, Thomas 146
FILSON, John 149
FORBES, Hugh 100 111 159
FORBIS, Capt 21 111-112 159
FORDICE, Samuel 145
FOREMAN, 125 William 37
FOUTS, Dave 80
GARRISON, George 146
GERMAN, William 145

GIRTY, Simon 78 152
GLASGOW, Stephen 146
GRAHAM, A A 137
GRAY, Thomas 145
GREATHOUSE, Jacob 8
GRINDSTAFF, Adam 145
GRIST, John 145
GROOP, Zebulon 151
GUTHRIE, 129
HAHN, Samuel 152
HALL, Adam 146 John 145
HAMILTON, Daniel 100 182 John 156 182
HAMMOND, John 115
HARMAR, 6 31 74 89 150 Gen 15-16 155 Josiah 5 149
HARMER, Gen 8
HARRIS, Thaddeus 40-41 166
HARRISON, 92 Anna 148 William Henry 90 148
HARROD, 51-53 171 James 128 Levi 89 95 William 22 26 98 129 170 William Jr 26 49-51 98 128 William Sr 52 128
HASPER, Alexander 115
HAZLET, Col 161
HEARCEY, William 146
HEDGE, Elijah 145 Joseph 145
HEDGES, 83 92 162-163 Elijah 30 91 Joseph 142 Samuel 49-50 91 142 Silas 142
HENDRICKS, David 145
HENNEY, Mary Jane 137
HERROD, William 146
HESS, Rick 43
HINKLE, Joseph 7
HOFFMAN, 27-28 58 63 67 69 97 123-124 135 142-143 Mr 131
HOLLIDAY, John 20
HOLLISTER, 42 56 59-60 64 66 139 171 174 Jeremiah 49-50 54-55 62 83 95 99 138 Judge 59 66
HOLMES, Joseph 145

HOLMS, Isaac 145
HOOST, Mary Magdalena 98
HORN, William Franklin 169
HOWE, 96 186 Henry 130 132
HUBBELL, William 7
HUFFMAN, 97 Christian 97 David 97 George 97 Henry 97 John 97 Philip 97 Phillip 97 Rossbury 97 Rudolph 97
HUGHES, 80 Abe 79
HULL, Gen 90 136
HUNT, Abner 7
HUPP, John 92
INDIAN, Blue Jacket 5 31 150 Charey Wilkey 27 Charley Wilkey 59 66 75 101-102 118 120 Chief Logan 8 165 Cornplanter 10 Kayashuta 155 Little Turtle 5 31 150 152 Spicer 25
INNIS, Harry 147
IRVIN, Thomas 152 William 145
ISRAEL, Boone 58
JAMES, William 151
JENKINS, Capt 94 112
JINKENS, Joseph 146
JOHNSON, Jane 84 Sterling 85
JOLLY, John 145 William 145
JONES, Joseph 146 Meckle 146 William 78
KEENER, Elizabeth 96
KELLOR, John 145
KELLY, John 145
KENTON, 73 Simon 117-118
KERNS, Mathew 145
KIDD, Alexander 146
KINGSBURY, Col 7
KIRK, John 145
KIRKWOOD, 29 106 113 Capt 105 107 155 Robert 28 30 160 162 Sarah 161
KITTS, Mary 94-95
KLINE, Jacob 129

KNOX, 18-19 Henry 5 17 30 51 105 147 173 Sec 28 Sherman 39 Stacy 39-40
LAMASTERS, John 8 145
LASHLEY, Joseph 145
LATTY, Robert 79
LAUGHLIN, William 146
LECKEY, Howard 169
LEGG, 129
LINDLEY, Caleb 160 Demas 160 John 160 Levi 160
LINE, John 27-28 58 67 97-98 Joseph 97-98 Mary 98 Samuel 97-98 William 97-98
LINES, 97 John 129 Simon 145
LINN, John 108-109 113-114
LOCKWOOD, Benjamin 145
LOGAN, Benjamin 58
LOWE, Naomi 46
LUCAS, Benjamin 145
MARSHALL, Col 112-113
MARSHEL, 17 21-22 James 15-16 20 54 93-94 157 162
MARTIN, Elijah 145 Hannah 84-85
MASSIE, Nathaniel 62 90 117-118
MCARTHUR, 56 59 63-64 66-68 75 119-120 139 171 187 Duncan 27 55 58 60 62 74 89-90 92 101 117-118 129 135 140 170 183 John 89 Nancy 91
MCBRIDE, Christina 160 John 160
MCCARTHUR, 140
MCCOLLOCH, 65 68 Abraham 91 Elizabeth 91 George 27 58 64 83 91-92 124 135 142-143 George Jr 91 John 91 Samuel 91
MCCOLLOUGH, George 127
MCCONNEL, Maj 115
MCCOUN, 98 Abraham 129 Isaac 129 Joseph 98
MCCOWAN, 56 98 142 181 Abraham 27-28 58 98 Isaac 26 54 94 98 130 John 98 Joseph 98
MCCOY, William 146
MCCULLICK, 140

Index

MCCULLOCH, George 145 George Jr 92 181 George Sr 92 181
MCCULLOUGH, George 92 George Jr 181 George Sr 181
MCCUNE, 143
MCDANNEL, John 122
MCDONALD, 42 55 60 64 66 102 139 John 49-50 62 91 101 117-118 122 134 183 187 Nancy 91
MCDOWELL, Samuel 92 183
MCGARY, Hugh 58
MCGOWAN, 131
MCGRAW, Thomas 146
MCGUIRE, Francis 10 154 Thomas 154
MCINTYRE, David 133 Mr 135
MCKEAN, Thomas 154
MCKEON, 98 Isaac 122 134
MCKEOWN, 98 Isaac 110 112
MCKIERNAN, 55-56 60 63 68 133 171 George 50 120-121 John 49
MCKOWEN, John 98
MCKOWN, Samuel 98 William 98
MEEK, Joshua 145
MEEKS, Isaac 151
MERCER, George 145
MICHAUX, Andre 165-166
MIFFLIN, 21-22 Gov 15 87 89 118 Thomas 149
MILER, Adam 94
MILLER, 56 122 134 Adam 26 53-54 92-93 110 112 130 172 Catherine 93 Frederick 93 Henry 93 Jacob 93 Jacob Jr 93 Jacob Sr 92 John 93 Mary 93 Peter 93
MILLS, Edward 145 Thomas 10 145 153
MINER, William 129
MITCHELL, Alexander 152 James 152
MORGAN, Capt 81 John 145
MORRISON, William 145
MORROW, Margaret 99
MORTON, Thomas 145
MULLER, Jacob 92

MURRY, Michael 145
NEAL, Jane 136
NEVILLE, John 156 Presley 11 14 156
NICHOLS, Thomas 112 184
NICHOLSON, Joseph 44
OGLE, 83
OHARA, James 86
PARKMAN, Francis 20
PARR, 163 Stephen 78
PATTEN, James 151
PATTERSON, Joel 145
PATTON, David 146
PAUL, 155
PERRY, Braden 145
PEYATT, Robet 145
POLLYARD, Jonathan Sr 145
PURDIE, Daniel 145
PUTNAM, Ezra 151 Rufus 4 6 148 151
RAMSEY, Isaac 167
RANDOLPH, Beverly 4 30
RANKIN, Thomas 111
RANNELS, Thomas 145
RAWLINGS, William 145
REDICK, 17 158 David 16 157
RICHARDS, Thomas 145 152
RIDDLE, Elizabeth 100
RILEY, 9-10 30 Francis 9 153 155 Moses 9 Mrs 9 Ruth 153
    William 153
RITCHIE, Matthew 100
ROBINSON, Israel 145
RONEY, Hercules 89 118 James 89
ROOSEVELT, Theodore 6
ROSS, 129
RUBLES, David 87
RUTTER, 45 Carolyn 44 Victor 44
RYERSON, Mr 107 Thomas 51-52 168

Index

SAINTCLAIR, Arthur 4-5 17 31 Gen 150 161
SAMUEL, Line 97
SCARMAHORN, Joseph 145
SCHEMERHORN, John 9 Ruth 153
SCOTT, Arthur 82 James 145
SCOUTCHFIELD, Nathan 145
SCUTCHFIELD, William 145
SEALS, James 85 95
SEAMAN, Jonah 145
SECRIS, Susannah 159
SHAPTAW, John 93
SHAW, Thomas 151
SHEPHERD, 10 30 Col 9 21 28 53 74 111 David 8 49 51 70 105-106 144 161 170 182 William 145
SHOPTAUGH, 93
SHOPTAW, 55-56 131 142-143 171 Andrew 94 Catherine 94 Henry 94 John 26 49-50 54 93-94 110-113 130 170 172 John Iii 94 John Jr 93-94 John Sr 93 William 93-94 111
SHOPTO, 122-123 134
SIX, Philip 146
SKINNER, Richard 145
SLOAN, Joseph 145
SMITH, Daniel 159 Thomas 145 William 145
SPENCER, John 145
SPICER, William 160
STACEY, John 151 Philip 151
STEENROD, Briggs 29 145 Daniel 29
STEPHENS, Samuel 146
STEPHENSON, William 146
STITES, Benjamin 4 87 89
SULLIVAN, Elizabeth 77-78
SUTHERLAND, 135 Alexander 99 Barbara 98 Daniel 99 David 99 142 181 George 98-99 John 27 58 98-99 124 142 181 John Jr 99 John Sr 98 Margaret 99 181
SWAN, John 129
SWEARINGEN, Andrew 181 Drusilla 153

SWEARINGHAM, Andrew 92 181
SYKES, 83
SYMMES, Anna 148 John Cleve 4 John Cleves 148
TAROL, Daniel 145
TATE, 58 99 114 139 182 John 99 Mr 99
TAYLOR, John 145
TEAGARDEN, Elizabeth 87
TEGARDEN, Mary 88
TODD, John 58
TOMLINSON, 42 54 56 59 64-65 67-68 171 Abelard 50 125-126 133 Joseph 20 37 124-125 Samuel 37 49 124-126
TRIGG, Stephen 58
TUCKER, John 145 William 145
VANAMAN, Garet 100
VANBUSKIRK, Laurence 145
VANBUSKIRKE, Lawrence 155 Rebecca 155
VANEMAN, Andrew 100-101 Elizabeth 100 Garrett 100 George 100 Nicholas 99-100
VANEMMAN, George 100
VANEMON, Andrew 100
VANMETER, Joseph 30
VANMETRE, Henry 129 John 129 Joseph 145
VANSWEARINGEN, Capt 70
VENEMON, Andrew 100 George 100
VENEMS, George 100
VENNAM, 75 Ray 27 58 65 99 101 135
VENNEMAN, Andrew 100 Garrett 100 George 100 Nicholas 100
VENNOMS, George 100
VINEMAN, George 100
VINNEMAN, Andrew 100 George 100 Solomon 100 Widow 100
VIRGIN, 173 Brice 80 Reason 116 Rezin 78
WALKER, John 29-30 145 Mr 107
WALLACE, John 152
WARNOCK, Jacob 145 John 145

Index

WASHINGTON, 38 Gen 167 George 37 43-44 150 165 Pres 4 10 148 173
WAXLER, Michael 145
WAYNE, 153 Anthony 78 Gen 31 115 117
WEIR, Gen 187
WELMETH, Francis 145
WETZEL, 22 73 77 83 165 John 39 46 Martin 91 164-165
WHETSELL, John 145
WHITE, William 145
WHITEHILL, James 146
WHITTAKER, Elijah 152
WILKENS, John Jr 11
WILKINS, John Jr 156
WILLIAMS, 121 Charles 145 Hugh 146 John 120 125 William 145
WILLIAMSON, David 159 Jeremiah 145 Joshua 152 Moses 145
WILMOTH, Francis 145 Jeremiah 145
WILSON, Isaac 146 John 146
WIRE, Daniel 49 67 132
WISEMAN, William 152
WITHERS, Alexander 133
WOOD, Isaac 146
WOODS, Edward 146 Joseph 146 Robert 42
WRIGHT, Alexander 146
YOHO, Catherine 78 94 Henry 78 94 James 94 Johannes 94 John 49-50 58 69-70 113-114 175 Margaret 78 94 Mary 94-95 Peter 78 94
ZANE, 73 124 Ebenezer 91 Elizabeth 91 Silas 153

www.ingramcontent.com/pod-product-compliance
Lightning Source LLC
Chambersburg PA
CBHW070741160426
43192CB00009B/1525